# WHAT OTHERS ARE SAYING ABOUT *TALENT FORCE!*

"*Talent Force* should be read by every executive! It drives home the single most important message—recruiting top talent is a continuous process that demands the same attention as any other key business process."

—**Bob Stutz,** Senior Vice President, CRM Global Strategy and Product

"There are a lot of books that address this very important business issue. In *Talent Force,* Rusty and Hank uniquely bring the effective use of technology into the picture. Their practical yet proactive approach is a must read for the 21st-century business leaders."

—**Aylwin Lewis,** President and CEO, Sears Holding Corporation

"In the global war for talent, the role of an aligned and collaborative economic and workforce agenda is critical for U.S. competitiveness and innovation capacity-building. *Talent Force* simply and elegantly describes the importance of human capital from the perspective of two individuals often on the front lines ensuring their clients and Corporate America are prepared with the right assets of skills and competencies. Rueff and Stringer should be at every table where a discussion is occurring about aligning an industry-driven perspective of C-Level Executives, HR, VPs of research and production, economic development specialists, policy-makers, and the public workforce system!"

—**Richard Seline,** CEO, New Economy Strategies, LLL, and former Deputy Assistant Secretary of U.S. Department of Commerce

"By introducing us to the new terms Talent Force and Q-Talent, Hank and Rusty take the talent industry to the next level. *Talent Force* is a straightforward and timely message that everyone, recruiter to CEO to candidate, should read as soon as possible."

—**Robert McNabb,** Executive Vice President, Korn/Ferry International; CEO, Futurestep

"Are you creating a talent crisis in your company? Wake up to a great new focus on Quality Talent. Mr. Stringer and Mr. Rueff provide exceptional thought leadership in this most critical personnel area."

—**Marty Seyer,** Corporate Vice President/General Manager, Commercial Business, Advanced Micro Devices (AMD)

"Fundamentally, business is human. *Talent Force* is the most current and powerful roadmap I have seen that translates your most critical asset—people—into bottom-line performance. This is both a deep and easy read that you should not only buy for yourself, but for all your friends who are leading in today's business world."

—**Keith Ferrazzi,** CEO, Ferrazzi Greenlight, and author of *Never Eat Alone*

"As the energy industry (utilities) anticipates a daunting exodus of retiring experienced craft workers, field workers, and engineers, we must overhaul our strategies to compete for, retain, and train the next generation of talent. The authors provide a very practical formula and framework for evaluating and competing for scarce labor in the talent market."

—**Fred Newton,** EVP & Chief Administrative Officer, Cinergy Corporation

"A must-read for any CEO or HR executive interested in actually measuring the effectiveness of their talent pool and gaining a huge competitive advantage."

—**Debbie McGrath,** CEO, HR.com

"Talent has always been the foundation of great companies, and nobody understands this more than Rusty Rueff. He has been a pioneer in talent acquisition and management for years and in this book shares a compelling viewpoint on the evolving challenges and strategies for winning the talent war."

—**Gregg Dedrick,** President and Chief Concept Officer, KFC

"Simple yet powerful. With many years of experience in the recruiting and talent arena, I was surprised that the content struck me with such impact. A new view into today's global talent market."

—**Darren Romano,** Partner, Global Practice Leader; Human Resources, Highland Partners

"Finding a way to motivate and keep talent *in* is the most important strategic issue of our time—this book deals with it head on. Its real, practical, and opens your mind to all the key issues; it's a must-read!"

—**Sahar Hashemi,** Founder, Coffee Republic

"As a leadership consultant and adviser to CEOs and Senior Leaders of over 200 Fortune 500 companies, I see organizations that develop a strategy of talent management consistently outperform their competitors. Superior talent is hard to find, recruit, and retain in any firm, but it holds the key to long-term success. With the innovative lessons from *Talent Force,* any leader can create a practical and proven approach to building their team with the best talent available."

—**Jim Hart,** President and CEO, Senn Delaney Leadership

"As both an executive for 20 years and now as an executive recruiter, the best hires are always the ones that you have proactively developed a deeper relationship with over time. This book provides a very practical guide to proactive recruiting at all levels that will distinguish the leading companies of the next generation.

—**Jerry Noonan,** Partner, Spencer Stuart

"The talent requirements to succeed in the new global economy are daunting. Smart companies will make talent their core asset. Those who don't...won't exist in the new global economy. *Talent Force* lays out a simple but effective game plan for building high-quality organizations. It's a must-read for line managers of all levels."

—**Dan Walker,** former Chief Talent Officer, Apple Computer, Inc.

"I've known Hank for a few years and he is clearly passionate about talent, whether it's finding it, recruiting it, or keeping it. Building a private talent community has become an essential business strategy and this book tells you the why and the how of all aspects of talenteering. A highly recommended book for CEOs, heads of HR, and professional recruiters."

—**Alan Jarvis,** Head of Global eHR Solutions, Allianz AG

"Business executives that see people as nothing more than a means to an end eventually fail. For the latter, they need to read *Talent Force*— soon!"

—**Brian Sommer,** President and Technology Analyst, TechVentive

"Q-Talent—it's what every organization covets but few know how best to get and keep. *Talent Force* will raise every expectation you have of your staffing department and change your thinking about talent management in general. You'll quickly see what can be done—and unfortunately what you're likely not getting done now. The good news is that the guidance given here will help you fill that gap with creative, but practical tactics needed for talent acquisition *now*. Read it and be prepared to change your approach to staffing and development on the spot."

—**John Murabito,** Chief Personnel Officer, Cigna Insurance

"Rusty Rueff and Hank Stringer deliver a blueprint to ensure that your organization will have the proper talent within a click of the mouse at all times. The difference between being proactive and reactive in acquiring talent can be the difference between business survival and failure. This book gives sage advice about how to aggressively and continually find the best people to work for your company."

—**Richard A. Cosier,** Dean and Leeds Professor of Management, Krannert School of Management, Purdue University

"Hank Stringer is a visionary and an evangelist for ensuring organizations are able to source the 'right' talent. In teaming up with Rusty Ruff from Electronic Arts, they have produced a 'must-read' for any CEO or head of talent in any organization that is serious about going beyond the bottom line."

—**Andrew Norton,** General Manager, HR, Auckland District Health Board

"In most things, if you always do what you always did, you'll always get what you always got. *Talent Force* is a guide to how to jump to the next level and how to see talent as the competitive edge."

—**Deval Patrick,** former senior executive, Texaco and Coca-Cola

"Some people just have recruiting in their bones, and Rusty Rueff and Hank Stringer, co-authors of this fine theoretical and practical how-to guide, are clearly two of them. Read it to find out why and how you have to create your new workforce starting today and moving into the future. Or don't read it and retire."

—**Bill Kutik,** Technology Columnist, *Human Resource Executive*

"This forward-thinking book, grounded in creative and practical application, is a must-read for any executive who is, or should be, concerned with creating a competitive advantage by recruiting and retaining top talent. *Talent Force: A New Manifesto for the Human Side of Business* delivers with breakthrough thoughts and solutions into building a global human capital business strategy."

—**John Malanowski,** Vice President, Talent Acquisition and Corporate Human Resources, Raytheon (John's global talent acquisition strategies are highlighted in the book)

"Like any marketing activity, talent management requires a life-cycle view. From understanding the demographics and behavior of potential employees through managing the friendliness of the hiring process, *Talent Force* provides guidance and encouragement. It is what the subtitle suggests: a manifesto for a new way of doing things. Thank goodness it's here now that we need it."

—**John Sumser,** CEO, Interbiznet

# TALENT FORCE

# TALENT FORCE

## A NEW MANIFESTO FOR THE
## HUMAN SIDE OF BUSINESS

Hank Stringer
Rusty Rueff

PEARSON
Prentice
Hall

Vice President and Editor-in-Chief: Tim Moore
Acquisitions Editor: Paula Sinnott
Editorial Assistant: Susie Abraham
Development Editor: Russ Hall
Director of Marketing: John Pierce
International Marketing Manager: Tim Galligan
Cover Designer: Chuti Prasertsith
Managing Editor: Gina Kanouse
Project Editor: Kayla Dugger
Copy Editor: Keith Cline
Senior Indexer: Cheryl Lenser
Compositor: Interactive Composition Corporation
Manufacturing Buyer: Dan Uhrig

© 2006 by Rusty Rueff and Hank Stringer
Publishing as Prentice Hall
Upper Saddle River, New Jersey 07458

**Prentice Hall offers excellent discounts on this book when ordered
in quantity for bulk purchases or special sales. For more information,
please contact U.S. Corporate and Government Sales, 1-800-382-3419,
corpsales@pearsontechgroup.com. For sales outside the U.S., please contact
International Sales, 1-317-581-3793, international@pearsontechgroup.com.**

Company and product names mentioned herein are the trademarks or registered
trademarks of their respective owners.

Printed in the United States of America

First Printing

ISBN 0-13-185523-9

Pearson Education LTD.
Pearson Education Australia PTY, Limited.
Pearson Education Singapore, Pte. Ltd.
Pearson Education North Asia, Ltd.
Pearson Education Canada, Ltd.
Pearson Educatión de Mexico, S.A. de C.V.
Pearson Education—Japan
Pearson Education Malaysia, Pte. Ltd.

**Library of Congress Cataloging-in-Publication Data**

Stringer, Hank.
    A new manifesto for the human side of business / by Hank Stringer
and Rusty Rueff.
        p. cm.
    ISBN 0-13-185523-9
    1. Manpower planning. 2. Employees—Recruiting. 3. Employee
retention.    I. Rueff, Rusty. II. Title.
HF5549.5.M3S745 2006
658.3—dc22

                                                        2005020538

*In dedication to the people around the globe who work hard to make themselves and their companies the best they can be, and who know they are more than workers . . . they know they are "talent."*

# TABLE OF CONTENTS

# FOREWORD

No leader achieves anything of true, lasting value alone. Whatever great things you aim to accomplish, whatever changes you're determined to drive, you need others to make it happen: others *working together in teams*. Therefore, building great teams ought to be your highest priority.

(That really ought to be self-evident. Sadly, though, I've seen plenty of organizations where it's not. Those organizations fail: nowadays, sooner, rather than later.)

Given their importance, how do you develop great teams? What are the foundational elements central to success?

To begin with, great teams require talented individuals who have the specific skills and know-how to get the job done. They must receive the resources they need: money, people, time, executive support. They need strong feedback mechanisms so they can track results in real time and quickly make course corrections. Finally, great teams must be empowered with the freedom and flexibility to find and execute great solutions—and do it *now*.

Makes sense, right? But I've barely alluded to the most important element. *You need outstanding people.* In the right roles. With a passion for owning the results.

Let's face it. Leaders really only empower people they believe in: people with the attitude, skills, leadership, and persistence needed for success.

And there's the rub: *there's more competition than ever before for the kind of people you CAN believe in.* It's increasingly challenging to find and recruit those scarce individuals. Even after you've brought them aboard, or developed them internally, talented people have a world of choices— *and they know it.* How do you keep them?

These are urgent questions. You need to address them head on. Reading *Talent Force* is an excellent way to start. Rusty Rueff and Hank Stringer crystallize the profound issues surrounding talent recruitment and management. Their book is far more than a manifesto. It offers powerfully innovative solutions, with real case studies to support them.

When I had the privilege of leading PepsiCo, I came to know Rusty as one of our most talented HR executives—and as a master recruiter. We're several years down the road, yet I can see the origins of many of this book's great ideas in his work for us at PepsiCo.

As our Vice President of International HR, he took on one of our most urgent challenges: finding people with outstanding international experience to support our global expansion. He systematically identified and built relationships with the best general managers throughout Asia, Europe, India, and Latin America: people who'd never worked with us, never even considered us. We found some of our best people that way. In fact, Rueff introduced me personally to a leader with such exceptional talent that we created a top position in China specifically for that individual.

When Rusty Rueff talks about the importance of building a *talent web*—a global community of talent you can draw on whenever the need arises—he's been there, done that, and demonstrated the results. When he talks about the importance of "high-touch" approaches in recruitment and retention, he's in a position to know.

When Hank Stringer talks about creating "talent brands" that encourage great people to come to you, or re-envisioning talent management for today's radically new business environment, or using the Web for more than just collecting resumés, it's not just talk. Hank, like Rusty, has been there—whether creating compelling recruiting brand messages for an up-and-coming computer company called Dell Computer, or innovating revolutionary Internet recruitment technology at Hire.com for companies the world over. Rueff and Stringer are talent experts; they've been out there doing these things, refining them, making them work, driving real business value.

Back at PepsiCo, we liked to say that the soft stuff is always harder than the hard stuff. The trick, we realized, was to make the soft stuff "hard": to operationalize it. When it comes to recruiting great people, *Talent Force* will help you do precisely that. If you're as committed to finding and nurturing great talent as I am, you'll find it invaluable.

Roger Enrico, Executive Chairman, DreamWorks Animation SKG;
and former Chairman and Chief Executive Officer, PepsiCo, Inc.
November 2005

# ACKNOWLEDGMENTS

I would like to acknowledge the following people who had an influence on this book, whether they knew it or not: Adrian Cheney at Pratt & Whitney, who would read me passages from *Atlas Shrugged* in our weekly one-on-one meetings to show me that work was more than one-dimensional; to Dave Zemelman, who took me under his wing at Frito-Lay to show me how to do his job someday; to Larry Probst, who had the courage to bring me from a big consumer packaged goods company to EA (a small interactive entertainment company at the time) to do a job that no one had done before for him; to my mother, Billie DeWees, who believed in my talent and instilled my work ethic in me; and to my wife Patti Rueff, who never once said, "Are you really spending all this time writing a book?"

—Rusty Rueff

I would like to acknowledge the following people who had an influence on this book, starting with every talented recruiter and candidate I have worked with in the past 25 years: from my friends early in my career at Diversified Human Resources, to Sally Pedley, who was willing to give me a chance at Tandem and embraced our use of the Internet in the early days to recruit quality talent; to Sam Gassett, who did the same at Dell and gave me the wonderful opportunity to recruit top talent for the company all over the world; and to every employee, client, and candidate who has worked with Hire.com—you changed the world! I am most thankful and blessed to have crossed paths and worked with "The Master of Talent" Jim Hammock, for without his influence, friendship, and guidance, this book would not have been possible. And special thanks to my good friends John Sumser, Kevin Wheeler, and Bill Kutik, the voices of the talent industry; thank you for your willingness to share. Your writing and speaking may be your work, but it is your passion that I so admire. Lastly and most importantly, thanks to the loves in my life; my wife Liz, the rock in my life, and to my children, Ryman and Jack, who give me so many daily joys and blessings.

—Hank Stringer

Together, we would like to acknowledge the talent who helped, herded, and edited us through this new process: Kelli Jerome, Paula Sinnott, Larry Heikell, Andrea Carlos, Anne Schott, Kayla Dugger, and Angela Wiley. A great team willing to gently nudge and politely suggest . . . we appreciate your wisdom, patience, and passion for this project. Thanks all!

# ABOUT THE AUTHORS

**Hank Stringer**
*Chief Executive Officer, Q Talent Partners*

Hank Stringer has over two decades of experience as a successful high-tech industry recruiter, entrepreneur, and innovator in the use of information technology in the recruitment and employment process. Today, Stringer is CEO of Q Talent Partners, an executive search services and consulting firm based on the philosophies and best practices of this book.

Forecasting a talent shortage in 1996, Stringer applied his energy and experiences to start Hire.com. There, he and a team of entrepreneurs created an early ASP business model, utilizing the Internet to scale and automate interactive recruiting relationships and processes. Under his tenure, Hire.com dramatically changed the way companies recruit, hire, and retain talent. Today, global companies, such as Federal Express, BP, Allianz, Raytheon, and Prudential, have adopted Hire.com's revolutionary approach.

Prior to founding Hire.com, Stringer was president and co-founder of Pedley-Stringer, Inc., a high-tech recruitment firm. Stringer previously served as an internal recruiting consultant for Tandem Computers and Dell Computer, where he was responsible for a number of special recruiting projects in the U.S. and Asia.

Stringer has authored many articles about recruitment and the future of talent management in the workplace, and is an accomplished speaker who has appeared at numerous international industry-leading events.

Stringer holds a B.A. in Journalism and Government Studies from Texas State University and currently serves as President of the Advisory Board for the McCoy School of Business at his alma mater. Hank resides with his wife and kids in the hill country outside Austin, Texas.

**Rusty Rueff**
*Chief Executive Officer, SNOCAP, Inc.*

Rusty Rueff joined SNOCAP as their CEO in 2005. SNOCAP is the world's first end-to-end solution for digital licensing and copyright management services, enabling record labels and individual artists to make the full depth of their catalogs available through authorized peer-to-peer networks and online retailers.

Prior to his position at SNOCAP, he was Executive Vice President of Human Resources for Electronic Arts (EA). Joining EA in 1998, he was responsible for global human resources, talent management, corporate services and facilities, corporate communications, and government affairs, reporting to EA's Chairman and CEO. EA is the world's largest, and leading, interactive entertainment software company, with revenues of over $3.5 billion and 6,500 employees. In 2003, *Fortune* named EA one of the "Top 100 Places to Work For" in the United States.

Prior to joining EA, Rueff held positions with the PepsiCo companies for over 10 years. He concluded his career with PepsiCo as Vice President, International Human Resources.

Prior to his tenure with PepsiCo, Rueff spent two years with the Pratt & Whitney Division of United Technologies. In addition, he spent six years in commercial radio as an on-air personality.

He holds an M.S. degree in Counseling and a B.A. degree in Radio and Television from Purdue University. He was given the honor in 2003 of being named a Distinguished Purdue Alumni. Rueff and his wife are the named benefactors of Purdue's Patti and Rusty Rueff Department of Visual and Performing Arts.

He currently serves on the Corporate Boards of SNOCAP, All Covered, and Sports Potential. He is on the Executive Committee of the Board of Trustees of San Francisco-based American Conservatory Theater (ACT). He is the majority owner of R-Squared Stables, based at Churchill Downs in Louisville, KY., and a member of the Academy of Television Arts & Sciences (ATAS). He and his wife, Patti, reside in Hillsborough, CA.

# PREFACE

A few years ago, we started talking every Wednesday—two executives, two former recruiters—just talking for an hour, an hour and a half, with no agenda, because we share many of the same values and are passionate about what we do. During these discussions, we kept coming back to the same topics: the changing employment landscape and innovative ways that organizations are responding to build their talent capital. After a while, we decided: Someone needs to go out and say some of these things, because it's time. These ideas are so important that they should be shared with a broader audience.

In case you are looking for it, this is not a manual. This is not the book for a person who is looking for a checklist or a recipe or the next initiative to launch on Monday. In the spirit of James C. Collins and Jerry I. Porras's book, *Built to Last*, we are not attempting to tell you what time it is or make you a time-teller, but instead to give you the raw materials and the tools to build your own clock.

What we have tried to do is write an "easy read," a simple book with powerful ideas that provokes your own insights and provides a framework that you can apply to almost any organization. We hope it helps you build relationships with your prospects and talent communities, get ahead of your sourcing needs, avoid the inefficiencies of the traditional "reactive" approach to recruiting and, ultimately, put the right person in the right place at the right time, all the time.

Rusty Rueff, Hillsborough, California
Hank Stringer, Austin, Texas
January 2006

# INTRODUCTION

"Like everyone else, I've got the same trucks. Like everyone else, I've got the same potatoes. Like everyone else, I've got the same machinery. The only thing I can have different is better people."

—Herman Lay, founder of the H.W. Lay Company,
later to become Frito-Lay, Inc.

Your company might have 10, 50, 500, 1,000, or 20,000 people, but do you have the right talent in the right places at every key position in your company? Do you see your employees not as a collection of bodies, but as the best collection of talent for your business? In short, do you have a workforce or a *talent force?*

Over the past 150 years, the Industrial Revolution, the exploding services industry, and three decades of business technology have transformed the workplace. Some jobs have gone the way of buggy builders and elevator operators, whereas giant new industries have emerged around new needs and new technologies.

How have companies faced these changes, embraced new challenges, and prospered? Talent—people making smart decisions, solving problems, pulling together, and believing in something. What differentiates your company is not your market position or your brand recognition. It is not even your products. It is the talent that drives all of those things. Quality talent (Q-Talent) within any organization has always been the key competitive differentiator.

Whether your ERP systems were designed by Oracle, SAP, or PeopleSoft; whether your trucks were built by Volvo, Isuzu, or Ford; whether your back-hoes were made by Caterpillar or Komatsu; the true competitive difference for all companies is the talent that pushes the business forward.

This book is about how to find, attract, and retain high-quality talent in the midst of a new, global economy that makes it more difficult and more important than ever to have the best possible people contributing to your organization. It is about how technology is changing the ways that both individuals and companies approach the job market. It is about how these forces and others will shape the talent market during the next decade and beyond and what smart companies will do to stay ahead. Most importantly, it is about the human factor involved in all of this and how expectations, views, and approaches to work are changing for participants in today's talent market.

The topic of talent is bigger than business. Talent is about who we are and goes to the core of what each one of us can contribute to the world. Do you know what you're good at, what you enjoy doing, and do you contribute these talents to your organization, your family, your team, or community every day?

---

### The Parable of the Talents

The concept of "talent" goes back a long way. The origins of the word *talent* lie with currency. Although estimates vary, in Biblical times, a talent was probably about 75 pounds of gold—a hefty sum that both bankers and chiropractors could appreciate.

One of the first glimpses into our modern understanding of talent appears in the Bible in the book of Matthew (25:14–30). In the "Parable of the Talents," three servants are each given a different number of talents by their master in accordance with each servant's ability. The first two put their talents to work immediately, made investments, and eventually doubled their sums. The third, fearful of failure, buried his talents in the ground.

Upon reporting back to the master, the first servant had turned his 5 talents into 10. The second servant had turned his 2 talents into 4. But the third servant still had only 1 talent, the one he had buried in the ground. Upset, angry, and disappointed with this lackluster return, the master ordered the third servant thrown "outside, where there will be weeping and gnashing of teeth."

This might sound like a simple reorganization of investment fund managers, but it is easy to see how this parable helped shape our understanding of the concept of talent, and subsequently, how the word itself acquired its modern meaning. Whether your talent is singing, sewing, calculus, or mergers and acquisitions, you have a choice to make—you can either take your talent out into the world and make something of it, or you can listen to your nagging fear of failure and stow it in the ground. Fate plays the role of master, rewarding those who develop their talents and taking away from those who do not.

This book takes the concept of talent beyond the individual to communities, companies, and even nations. As a leader in any setting, the more you work to recognize, attain, nurture, and develop the spectrum of talent in your organization, the more the organization will realize its potential and the more successful it will be.

On a more pragmatic level, this book addresses some real-world business issues, such as the following:

- Building a new, more effective talent organization that knows how to find and attract *quality* talent quickly and build new forms of value for the business along the way

- Putting a solid talent plan in place that aligns with business objectives

- Creating a talent brand that communicates your company's value and attracts the types of candidates you desire

- Using technology, effective communications, and imagination to build large talent communities, generate efficiency in your hiring process, and tap into new sources of competitive intelligence, promotional opportunities, and even new revenue streams

- Measuring talent acquisition and retention efforts so that you can more effectively understand and respond to your talent needs

- Understanding how candidates are using technology to find opportunities, learn about companies, benchmark their compensation and communicate with one another about work life—and how you should respond

- Looking at new ways that companies and candidates will communicate with one another, both in the mass media and with advanced communications technologies

Along the way, *Talent Force* discusses these issues, which describe developments and challenges in managing talent capital:

- Quality talent is always scarce. Having the right talent in the right place at the right time is a make-or-break factor for organizations of all sizes—companies and nations alike.

- Evolving demographics, technologies, and economies create both challenges and opportunities for finding the best talent.

- Companies develop their strategic recruiting capabilities and a new type of recruiter emerges at the corporate-strategy and operational levels. This role becomes a critical component of any competitive business.

- The quest for better jobs becomes a public obsession. Talent is recruited at every opportunity. It takes a finely tuned and targeted talent brand to cut through the clutter.

- Everyone is available all the time, waiting for that next opportunity to come along and capture his or her attention. The Web is the recruiting weapon of choice.

- Smart companies realize a competitive advantage by measuring their talent efforts to help them improve. Shareholders, analysts, and business leaders factor new talent measurements into investment strategies and policy decisions. State and local governments explore talent-oriented economic programs.

- Like high-value free agents, talent can and will articulate its worth. Companies now have the burden of putting up or losing out.

- Even with an online talent community of millions—a group of prospective candidates who have expressed interest in your organization—relationship recruiting remains a competitive advantage and differentiator. Talent must still have a name and a face for you to win them over. Continuous recruitment is required not only to attract the next generation of Q-Talent, but also to retain your existing Q-Talent.

- Changes in behavior, technology, demographics, natural resources, and other areas force businesses to continually look ahead and adapt. Wherever talent scarcity takes hold, recruiting innovation responds. The most competitive organizations will be leaders in this space.

- If you are a CEO, this book is required reading. It will give you the conceptual framework to push a strategic agenda with your human resources leaders and hiring managers and new ideas to position your company for growth in any economy.

- If you are a hiring manager, this book will help you see the big picture in planning for your talent needs, filling in the holes on your team, and getting the most out of each and every hire. It will help you understand the pent-up demand for jobs that has been on hold during the economic slowdown and help you get a leg up in retaining your top performers when the climate improves.

- If you are a job seeker, this book shows you how to be more competitive in the marketplace and how to put yourself on a path toward your dream job, armed with the understanding you need to take full advantage of the opportunities that lie ahead.

- And for HR professionals, this book is nothing less than the future of your profession. Put it down and you might just get left behind.

*Talent Force* represents a huge opportunity for companies to build something that their competitors do not have. The choice is yours. The future is now. Are you ready?

| | NEW FORCES AT WORK | |
|---|---|---|
| | WORK FORCE ⟶ | TALENT FORCE |
| TALENT SUPPLY | Arrogance of Supply | Quality Talent is Always Scarce |
| TECHNOLOGY | Manual | Always On - Always Available |
| | Search & Retrieve | A Keystroke Away |
| TALENT ATTITUDES | Employer in Control | Shared Employer/Employee Control |
| | Work is Compartmentalized | Work is a Cultural Obsession |
| DEMOGRAPHICS | Local Sourcing | Global Sourcing |
| | Stable | Dynamic Shifts |
| | Homogeneous | Diverse & Aging |
| ECONOMICS | Assumptions, "Soft" Metrics | "Hard" Valuations |
| | Cost Center | Contributes Directly to Bottom Line |
| GLOBALIZATION | Work Done Within Borders | Dispersed Work & Talent Base |
| | Work Done By Locals | Immigrating & Emigrating Talent |
| RECRUITERS | Process Management | Holistic Employment Brand Management |
| | Order-Taking | Proactive Planning, Secure Talent Ahead of Demand |
| | Lassiez-Faire | Speed – Accountability |
| | Manual/Individual Tracking | Technology Savvy, Scalable, Long-term Systems |
| | Information Provider, Evangelist | Organizations-wide Selling Strategist & Leader |
| MARKETING | Short-sighted | Strategic, Compelling |
| | No Investment | Investment with Measured Returns |
| | Non-aligned with Corporate Messaging | Talent Brand, Aligned with Corporate Messaging |

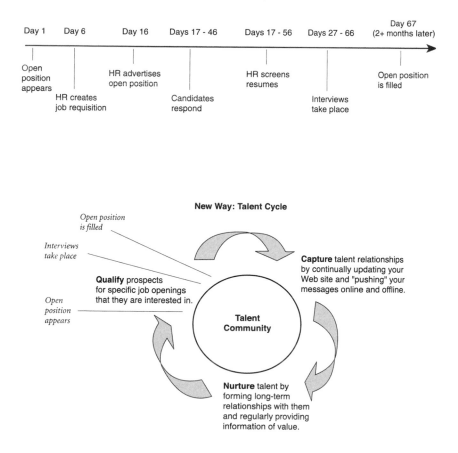

**Old Way: Linear Talent Acquisition**

| Day 1 | Day 6 | Day 16 | Days 17 - 46 | Days 17 - 56 | Days 27 - 66 | Day 67 (2+ months later) |
|---|---|---|---|---|---|---|

Open position appears

HR creates job requisition

HR advertises open position

Candidates respond

HR screens resumes

Interviews take place

Open position is filled

**New Way: Talent Cycle**

Open position is filled

Interviews take place

Open position appears

**Qualify** prospects for specific job openings that they are interested in.

**Capture** talent relationships by continually updating your Web site and "pushing" your messages online and offline.

**Talent Community**

**Nurture** talent by forming long-term relationships with them and regularly providing information of value.

# 1

# THE QUALITY TALENT
# IMPERATIVE

---

*Forces in Play:* Quality talent is always scarce. Having the right talent in the right place at the right time is a make-or-break factor for entities of all types and sizes—companies and nations alike.

"We're under-investing in the business because of the limitations of hiring . . . We are unquestionably not getting the quantity of top applicants that the company seeks."

—Sergey Brin, Google co-founder, at the company's first analyst conference on February 9, 2005

Quality talent is always scarce. Even during the employers' market of the past 50 years, there has been—and always will be—a shortage of quality talent. Think about it. Do your colleagues, directors, and managers—each one of them—continuously exceed expectations? Have you turned away ideal job candidates because your organization already overflows with stellar talent? When a new opportunity arises, is a highly qualified person immediately available to embrace it? No leader of any company, country, or economy has ever claimed that his people are just too effective and that he does not know what to do with all of their skills.

When you internalize the fact that there is always a shortage of quality talent, you can plan accordingly. When former General Electric Company chairman Jack Welch retired in 2000, there were several excellent potential successors inside of his executive branch. He picked his successor, and those who were not selected either retired or became company leaders elsewhere.

The departure of those who were not chosen to succeed Welch might seem like a backfire of sorts, but it shows that GE "gets it"—there is always a shortage of quality talent, so they planned and invested to have a deep bench of executives available when needed. This bench of senior leaders had been well trained, groomed, and developed. Each was capable of running the company. They were CEOs in the making, and in waiting.

---

**Migration of CEO-Level Talent from GE**

The following list shows the track record of some GE executives who were being readied for the CEO position from 2000 to 2004, when there was CEO succession:

|  | 2000 | 2004 |
|---|---|---|
| Jack Welch | Chairman and CEO | Retired |
| Jeff Immelt | Senior VP, GE Medical Systems | Chairman and CEO, GE |

| Lewis Edelheit | Senior VP, R&D | Retired; serves on multiple advisory boards and boards of directors |
| --- | --- | --- |
| Lawrence Johnston | Senior VP, GE Appliances | Chairman and CEO, Albertson's, Inc. |
| James McNerney | Senior VP, GE Aircraft Engines | Chairman and CEO, 3M |
| Robert L. Nardelli | Senior VP, GE Power Systems | President, Chairman and CEO, Home Depot, Inc. |
| John D. Opie | Vice Chairman of the Board | Retired; serves on the boards of Delphi Corp. and Wal-Mart |
| Mike Zafirovski | Senior VP, GE Lighting | President and COO, Motorola |

This kind of depth at the executive level, or at any level, cannot occur without the belief that great people are always hard to find—and keep. And this depth of talent will never materialize without the processes to put that belief into action. GE had the belief and processes in place, making a critical difference to one of the most strategic elements of the company.

A 1995 article on the subject in *Fortune* magazine quoted the University of Michigan's Noel Tichy, who described GE's system for identifying and developing talent as "so comprehensive that it is rivaled only by the military." Tichy's observation was validated in the January 2005 issue of *BusinessWeek* magazine, which listed both Immelt and Nardelli, the latter in his new role as chairman of Home Depot, as part of its "Best Managers of the Year" feature. With a systematic, methodical approach, it is no wonder GE had half a dozen managers who were genuinely ready to lead the company.

This high-profile example features high-profile executives, but the quest for the best talent extends to all levels of an organization.

As previously stated, quality talent is always difficult to find. Here's another reality about talent: *At every level, quality talent matters.*

For your organization to thrive, you need quality talent in everyone from the CEO to the custodian. How many stories have we all heard about the clerk who rises to become head of a company or department? Not only does the clerk have great talent, so does the person who hired the clerk—with this hire, he has made an incalculable contribution to the business.

Where quality talent is lacking, organizations suffer. Middle-managers who focus too heavily on numbers rather than people can lead to systemic morale problems and lost productivity. Design flaws overlooked by an engineer can lead to costly recalls and extensive liability. Errors in accounting can lead to write-downs, sanctions, and unhappy investors. Inefficient drivers can waste fuel and increase overtime expenditures. Inattentive receptionists can lead to irritated clients checking their watches in your lobby. Dirty, wet floors can lead to accidents and lawsuits. Unmotivated clerks can lead to lost mail, or worse, bad coffee.

What do we mean by *quality* talent? Quality talent is valuable knowledge and skills applied to the needs of an organization. Quality talent is an experienced veteran who simply knows how to make things work, a savvy manager who can motivate and build consensus, a jovial co-worker who does her job well and keeps the team on an even keel, the receptionist who just knows how to keep everyone happy. Superstars such as these might comprise only a small percentage of the company, but if any of them left today, it would affect the business in ways you might not even realize. Sure, the vacated position can be filled, but how do you find another person with equal or greater talent in two weeks?

For purposes of this book, we will refer to quality talent going forward as *Q-Talent.*

At every level in the organization, finding, hiring, and retaining Q-Talent is a huge challenge, fraught with intangibles—and critical to success. The Q-Talent imperative will never go away, and those who get it right will always have an edge. The more you can put the right person with the right attitude, experience, and skills in the right place at the right time, the better off your business will be.

Before going further, let's look at how important it is to have the right people in the right place at the right time.

In this age of technology, after decades of relatively abundant labor, the value of individual human contributions has been commoditized in some places and trivialized in others. Computer programs, heavy machinery, and other technologies can quickly and easily do the work of many human beings. Arrogance of supply, the pervasive notion that there will always be another warm body to throw at problems and opportunities as they arise, has reigned. Often lost in this abundant quantity of workers has been a discerning eye for quality.

The reality is that it is not enough just to have a person in place. Only the right person with the right skills, attitude, and attributes can realize the potential of any given role at any given point in time. The reality is that the fate of nations and entire economies has hinged on the simple-sounding concept of "right person, right place, right time." The following are just a few examples. If you look for them, you can find these kinds of stories throughout human history.

## The Talent to Move a Nation

In the middle of the nineteenth century, one of the greatest U.S. presidents, Abraham Lincoln, acted on a vision to connect his vast country from east to west via railroad. To make this vision a reality, he needed strong backs and arms to drive the spikes and lay down the rails. Without heavy machinery, the entire line would have to be cleared, leveled, and graded using shovels, picks, black powder, and, quite literally, horsepower. The project required thousands of men with the skills, muscle, and work ethic to physically move mountains.

However, by 1865, the Central Pacific Railroad had five times as much work as it had laborers to perform it. Finding Q-Talent with the right skills to do the job was proving enormously problematic. In addition, turnover was high due to long hours, hard work, the peril associated with the "Old West," and the inherent difficulties of managing such a complex project. Creating an effective talent force had become one of the biggest obstacles to meeting this historic challenge.

At the same time, on the U.S. West Coast, due mostly to the 1849 California gold rush, a large population of Chinese immigrants had sprung up. After long, difficult stints in the mines seeking the Gum Sham, the "Mountain of Gold," many of these immigrants were taking whatever other jobs they could find. On the East Coast, waves of Irish immigrants had been arriving for decades, and thousands of Civil War soldiers and freed slaves shared their common need—wages.

The result? A vast, untapped, available talent force collided serendipitously with one of the most ambitious development projects in the history of mankind. Had this talent force not been available, one of the greatest accomplishments in U.S. history might never have happened.

The recruitment of Irish laborers, Civil War veterans, and freed slaves along the eastern seaboard provided the necessary brawn to get the project moving, but it was the influx of Chinese workers that single-handedly changed the complexion of this enormous undertaking. The Chinese workers brought a new cultural perspective and a fresh attitude. They were on time. They worked hard. They agreed to their compensation up front and stuck to those commitments while other groups held out for higher wages. They had a healthier diet than most of the Irish and American workers, too, incorporating vegetables and fish. They drank tea rather than water, which helped them avoid dysentery. Unlike many of their contemporaries, they bathed regularly, washed their clothes, and stayed away from alcohol. As any modern-day line manager knows, factors such as these can really add up when it comes to job performance.

Soon, labor recruiters were scouring California, and the railroad's primary contractor, Charles Crocker, began to advertise the work in the Canton province of China. Several thousand Chinese men signed on, and by 1868, they numbered more than 12,000, or roughly 80 percent of Central Pacific's talent force.

By this time, Central Pacific's teams had jelled into a precise, cohesive unit. On the other side of the country, the Union Pacific Railroad and its legions of men were also picking up steam. As the tracks drew closer, they began to converge at a rate of 7 to 9 miles per day—nearly as fast as a family could travel across the country using a team of oxen. Talk about an effective talent force! The talk today is about it being a "Flat World."

Indeed, we subscribe to Friedman's hypothesis. The example above is one where, for talent, the world began to flatten long before the technology revolution. Work has sought out, regardless of geography, Q-Talent, for a long time. It is now that we are clearly seeing the advancements due to the open global communication and information sharing.

In the end, this single project transformed a nation, and the ripples of that change touched most of the world. Before the transcontinental railroad, a trip from New York to San Francisco could take anywhere from six months to a year. After the railroad was complete, the trip took seven days. This accessibility has profoundly impacted the U.S. economy and every other country that depends on its products and resources.

# Zimbabwe's Displaced Agricultural Talent Force

In 2000, President Robert Mugabe of Zimbabwe mandated that, under his leadership, the country would take a dramatic step. White farmers who had been farming in the country for more than a century would be forced to give up their lands to the region's indigenous Africans. Mugabe insisted this step was necessary to reverse the effects of British colonialism, which had left whites in control of a majority of Zimbabwe's most fertile farmlands.

Enforced by a militia loosely known as "war veterans," who squatted on properties to harass and threaten the occupants into leaving, Mugabe's land-reclamation initiative largely achieved its goal.

However, during the struggle, several white farmers who had worked the land for generations were attacked and killed. Hundreds of millions of dollars in crops were either abandoned as farmers were forced to hastily relocate, or neglected as Mugabe's war veterans fought with the farmers and prevented workers from doing their jobs.

Not surprisingly, agricultural production plummeted immediately in a country once considered a breadbasket for the region. Once an exporter of maize, Zimbabwe began to face a dire maize shortage and could not import enough of it to keep up with demand. Mugabe blamed the crisis on a prolonged drought in the region, and his supporters dismissed any connection between the famine and the administration's policies, saying that the displaced white farmers had primarily grown tobacco.

The lost agricultural production threatened the entire region's population. Neighboring countries, such as Zambia and Malawi, depended on Zimbabwe for its exports of the staple crop maize since their own agricultural programs were on shaky ground. As many as 13 million people across Africa were affected by the sudden shortage. Many were starving.

Compounding the problem, these farms had employed thousands of people who suddenly found themselves without jobs. Some groups estimated that as many as 70,000 people were without work. In addition, much of the "redistributed" land was given not to farmers, but to high-ranking soldiers, diplomats, and other insiders who did not work the land to its capacity, leaving unfilled holes in agricultural production and employment.

Interestingly, several neighboring countries understood the value of this newly available pool of skilled talent. In Mozambique, where all farmland is owned by the government and leased to farmers, only 4 million of the country's estimated 36 million hectares of usable farmland were being utilized. Some displaced farmers moved there and leased farmland from the government. Angola, whose maize production was long stunted by civil war, recruited the unemployed Zimbabwean farmers to help increase output there. Officials in Malawi and Botswana encouraged the farmers to invest and form joint ventures with existing farmers in their countries. All of these countries opened their arms to the farmers in one way or another.

About 300 of the farmers settled just across the Zambezi River in neighboring Zambia. *The Economist* said it succinctly: "Zim's loss, Zam's gain." These former Zimbabwean farmers are now running about 150 farms in Zambia, many of which employ dozens or even hundreds of people. In 2004, for the first time since 1978, Zambia was able to export more corn than it imported. Nineteen thousand tons of that crop were sent to Zimbabwe.

And what about the claim by Mugabe's supporters that the displaced farmers primarily grew tobacco? It is estimated that about one third of the farms seized in Zimbabwe's land redistribution were growing primarily tobacco. In the year 2000, Zimbabwe, a powerhouse of tobacco production, produced a whopping 237,000 tons of the gold leaf. After that record crop, the country saw 4 straight years of decline until, in 2004, it produced an estimated 65,000 tons. Meanwhile, neighboring countries have become rising stars in tobacco production. From 2000 to 2004, Zambia's tobacco output increased fourfold.

In all, the displacement of a few thousand farm owners caused major shifts in the gross domestic product of several African countries, as well as dramatic fluctuations in the prosperity of entire populations.

## New Zealand's Muffled Boom

With a highly skilled population willing to work hard, stable agriculture, and thriving industry, New Zealand can weather almost any economic storm. The economic slowdown of the early millennium did not affect this southern country as harshly as many others. Soon on the rebound, New Zealand found itself experiencing a boom of sorts.

Good news? Most would say yes, but the growth required a massive expansion of infrastructure, which in turn depended on skilled construction labor. And there was not enough of that needed labor to do the work.

In May 2004, the headline from Auckland was direct: "Builders plead for help as workload crisis threatens projects." The threatened projects included vital public works, such as hospitals, schools, universities, and prisons. Already short 3,000 workers, Auckland's construction docket was slated to double in the next year, with $3.2 billion in work proposed. As a result, construction workers who were making $20NZ per hour in 2000 now commanded $32NZ, a 60 percent increase over 4 years. The rising costs had already forced some projects to redesign and others to scale back. Some apartment developers had even been forced to ask for more money on units already sold.

As a result, builders turned to the government for help in finding this vital talent force of construction workers, wherever in the world they were located, and in getting them to the job sites. Some companies even asked for governmental relief with their payrolls as wages skyrocketed.

The government has responded by offering incentives to expatriates who return home to work. New Zealand is also considering unique work visas for construction workers interested in visiting the country, which many consider the most beautiful in the world. As this example illustrates, the scarcity of Q-Talent can hinder progress, even an economic boom. To find Q-Talent, creative solutions, such as the ones that New Zealand's government introduced, are required.

If having the right talent in the right place at the right time can affect the fate of nations, how can it not affect your company and your industry? In fact, the people you need to solve your most pressing issues and embrace your greatest opportunities are not that different from the CEO of GE, railroad laborers in nineteenth-century America, farm workers in Zimbabwe, or construction workers in New Zealand. These people all represent Q-Talent, those who apply valuable knowledge and skills to the needs of a project, organization, or even a country.

Every organization that wants to remain competitive must create a plan to acquire the right talent and ensure that talent is available for the work that needs to be done today and in the future. The next chapter looks at major worldwide trends that you need to consider as you begin planning your organization's approach to acquiring and retaining Q-Talent.

# 2

# TALENT MARKET DEMANDS

---

***Forces in Play:*** *Evolving demographics, technologies, and economies create both challenges and opportunities for finding the best people.*

---

**B**efore you evaluate your specific need for Q-Talent and begin developing plans to acquire it, you need to understand how your approach will be—and perhaps already is—fundamentally affected by major changes and trends worldwide. Take a good look around. Look beyond your organization to what is happening in your community, but do not stop there. Look at what is happening across your country and around the globe.

This chapter explores five major, worldwide trends that will increasingly influence efforts to find and acquire Q-Talent: an aging workforce, young workers entering the workforce for the first time, immigration, offshoring, and emerging talent markets. This chapter also touches on two recruiting-specific trends: recruitment process outsourcing and talent measurement.

## The Only Constant Is Change

We have established one constant—the scarcity of Q-Talent. Another significant constant for business is change. Successful companies are always prepared for change because the ability to manage change is built into their cultures and their processes.

On a macro level, the world today faces dramatic changes. Cultural evolution, population changes, and economic shifts interact to create constant displacement and churn.

Population growth in developed nations has long been flat, whereas in many developing countries, the population is exploding. Technology has enabled broad information access, global communications, and synchronicity. Industrialized nations have moved toward a knowledge- and service-based economy while outsourcing many of their manufacturing activities. Combine all that with the establishment of free-trade zones, terrorism, the global rise of democracy, the influence of the media, higher prices for oil, and as many other factors as you can think of, and you begin to see the enormity of the changes facing the global economy. The mere fact that we now talk about "global economy" is a change.

As these macro forces converge, they will profoundly affect all aspects of talent—finding it, hiring it, developing it, and retaining it. Further, a shift will occur in the balance of power in the hiring equation. In some places, broad changes are already reshaping the traditional recruiting model in new ways. It is important to understand these changes so that you can begin to think differently about talent and plan to acquire and retain the talent you need to stay competitive.

Although many of these trends and conditions are new to us, the principles are not. Think of the dramatic changes in work and cultural life that occurred during the twentieth century and try to imagine what another 100 years will bring.

For example, at the beginning of the twentieth century in the United States, more than 30 percent of Americans worked on the farm. Today, less than 3 percent do. Over the span of a dozen decades, one of the largest economies in the world transformed from one based primarily on agriculture and natural resources, to one based on manufacturing and industry, to one based on information, management, and services.

Along the way, workers were displaced. Many were forced to move from their rural environments to urban industrial hubs. The ability to read and write took on new importance that it did not have on the farm. Literacy rates rose. New occupations and professions emerged. Children, women, and minority groups gained new rights and status.

With each generation, a new set of expectations arose. Kids did not want to become cobblers, coopers, blacksmiths, or stable tenders. They wanted to become factory workers, lawyers, scientists, and movie stars. Later, their kids wanted to become astronauts, athletes, consultants, and computer programmers. Each generation's talent wanted less dirt under their fingernails and more money in their pockets. Then, as now, there was no going back.

We have seen sweeping, worldwide economic changes before. We have seen technology send shockwaves across the world before. We have seen new industries and initiatives drive intense demand for certain skills—and have seen entire workforces compelled to provide them. The situation facing twenty-first–century business is unique, but the reality is that the global economy is constantly changing and evolving. And businesses and talent are constantly responding to these changes.

As was the case a century ago, new skills are required today. New types of careers are emerging. New types of talent are coveted and pursued. New talent pools are being found and tapped into. The supply of and demand for great talent—Q-Talent—is shifting from industry to industry, from region to region, and both people and companies are compelled to adapt. A major difference today is that the entire world can play the same game on an increasingly level playing field.

## Generational Change

Sweeping demographic changes at both ends of the generational spectrum are affecting the talent market in new ways. At one end, an aging workforce is shrinking the available pool of Q-Talent; at the other end, young workers entering the talent market for the first time are bringing priorities and expectations that need to be understood and addressed.

One of the most profound trends facing the talent arena is worldwide aging of the population in developed nations. In Japan, the labor force is expected to fall by 1.6 million persons by 2007, another million shy of where they were in the mid-1990s. Germany is expected to lose nearly half a million workers in the same time frame. Italy, too, is witnessing a slow and steady decline in its working-age population. U.S. Bureau of Labor Statistics projections show that the number of people 55 or older in the U.S. workforce will increase more than 49 percent by 2010, whereas the number of workers between the ages of 35 and 54 will increase only 5 percent.

In industrialized nations around the world, population growth is either flat or declining. In the top 50 industrial countries worldwide, mortality rates have been approaching or exceeding birth rates for years, creating a dwindling supply of new talent going into the next decade as the existing population continues to age. In the United States alone, Bureau of Labor Statistics data indicate a shortfall of 5 to 10 million workers as the twenty-first century moves through its second decade.

---

**Will the United States Experience a Labor Shortage?**

The U.S. Bureau of Labor Statistics cautions against predicting any labor shortage from its raw data. Too many variables are at stake, says the bureau, for simple arithmetic to resolve. Those who hold multiple jobs, for example, are not factored in. However, others have sounded the alarm. A 2001 study from the non-profit, U.S.-based Employment Policy Foundation points to a shortfall in the United States of 35 million workers by 2030, when nearly a quarter of the country's population will be over the age of 65.

Regardless of any possible shortfall in the number of "warm bodies" in any industrialized nation, few would argue that certain industries worldwide are headed toward a dire skills shortage. Medicine is one, along with other science-related disciplines. Countries and communities that can solve this labor shortage problem early and get more young people interested in acquiring the necessary skills will be well ahead of the curve.

For our part, we will repeat, there is *always* a shortage of Q-Talent. Consider this revealing statistic, also from the United States: According to the Employment Policy Foundation's July 2004 update, while overall unemployment in the United States hovered around 5.5 percent for individuals age 35 and older, for those with a 4-year degree or higher, the unemployment rate was 2.7 percent. For those with some college education but less than a 4-year degree, the unemployment rate in July 2004 was 4.2 percent. During the same period, for those with only a high school diploma, the unemployment rate was 5.1 percent, and the

---

unemployment rate for those who had not completed high school was 8.3 percent.

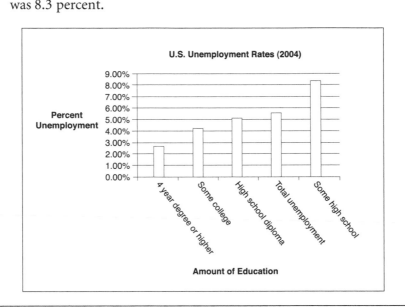

This data leads to two conclusions:

- The U.S. economy, as with many advanced nations, is increasingly geared toward educated workers with well-developed problem-solving and information-literacy skills. There are simply more opportunities for college-educated workers because the global economy has evolved in a direction that requires the abilities of a more educated workforce.

- With only 2.7 percent of college-educated workers unemployed in the United States in July 2004, these workers are already scarce, and competition for them is already a major challenge for organizations.

The message for job seekers is the same as it is always been: Stay in school, be it a two-year college, four-year university, or vocational institute. Develop your skills. The market for skilled, educated, high-quality talent is always competitive.

If the population in industrialized nations remains flat or declines, while the respective economies in those nations continue to grow, sooner or later a tipping point will occur.

The impact on the health-care industry alone will be huge over the next decades, as the "Baby Boom" generation (not just in the United States, but worldwide) surpasses 55 years of age, enters retirement, and eventually reaches old age. Hospitals, pharmaceutical companies, and health-care systems across the globe—already facing a shortage of great talent—will need more people to keep up with the demand that this demographic shift will place on their services. That means more facilities, staffed by more nurses, more doctors, more laboratory technicians, more nutritionists, more biochemists, and more janitors.

And that is just one industry. According to Kevin Wheeler, president of Global Learning Resources, the United States should also expect local shortages of talent in the technology, accounting, and finance industries and in positions requiring expertise in science or math.

These demographic shifts will also bring about changes in work habits, expectations, and lifestyle priorities. For example, many older workers, by will or by circumstance, will decide to work beyond traditional retirement age. The results of a February 2005 survey of U.S. adults found that 63 percent of those who have not yet retired predict that they will continue to work for pay in retirement. About a third said they would work to "stay busy," and about a quarter said they would need to continue working for the money.[1]

At the other end of the spectrum, younger generations, in addition to being fewer in number, will bring about a different set of changes. Every generation learns from its parents, world events, the socio-political environment, and from the technology and culture of its time. Joined by these factors, each generation in each culture makes a shift in its values, goals, work ethic, philosophy, and activities.

Today, the focus of younger generations might be on results over processes, friends more than family, and happiness as opposed to mere financial success. The generation after them, having never known a world without cell phones, global positioning, instant messaging, and the Internet, will have entirely different expectations for how business and social interactions take place.

---

[1] Source: *Ipsos-Public Affairs for the Associated Press,* http://www.ipsos-na.com/news/pressrelease.cfm?id=2593.

The global workforce is graying, and talent force demographics are shifting. To remain competitive, businesses and governments must consider how they are affected by both an aging population and the new priorities of young workers:

- What will happen when there is a burgeoning retirement and care industry?

  - More demand for pharmaceuticals

  - Fewer people able to stand on their feet 8 hours a day or lift 50-pound boxes

  - More people who would rather use their minds and their experience than their backs

  - More people wanting to work part-time

  - More readers of *AARP* magazine and fewer readers of *Maxim*

- What will be the defining attributes of the next generation of new talent?

- How will businesses accommodate, integrate, and balance the expectations of each generation, especially those of young workers entering the workforce for the first time?

- What innovative techniques can businesses employ to effectively tap into the talent market at both ends of the generational spectrum?

- How will perceptual differences among not only age groups, but cultures, subcultures, nationalities, and faiths, affect prospective workers on an individual level—and what should organizations do about it?

## Immigration

The September 11, 2001, terrorist attacks in the United States changed the way that all nations must deal with immigration. In the United States, where immigration is part of the national identity, heightened security has naturally led to tighter immigration laws, making it more difficult for U.S. companies to source talent from overseas. The process for obtaining a visa to study or work in the United States has become much more cumbersome. These facts alone can make it nearly impossible for transnational businesses to hold impromptu meetings, and can make it much more challenging to reel in top talent from abroad.

Something as simple as an immigration law prohibiting a spouse from working in the host country can quickly reduce a company's options when it comes to sourcing from abroad. As a result of the red tape, even if the employees are paid less, companies are generally spending more for those foreign workers than for domestic ones.

Take a moment now and think about the talent force in your company today versus a few years ago. Are there people working for you now whose original citizenship is not the same as yours? Are you having conversations about sourcing some of your products and services from other regions of the world? Do you wish that you and your management team spoke one, two, or more different languages? If none of this rings a bell, take a walk through the cafeteria and look at who is there. You might find that your talent force is diversifying without you fully realizing it. If immigration restrictions impede your efforts to get the diversified talent you need, how will your business be affected?

Tightened immigration has had a profound impact on education as well. Education determines the quality of a country's future workforce because students often remain in the country where they were educated. *Open Doors,* an annual publication on international educational exchange, reports a dramatic decrease in the growth rate of U.S. international student enrollment, from a growth rate of 5 percent in 1997–1998 to more than 6 percent in 2000–2001, then dwindling to a growth rate of less than 1 percent in 2002–2003. Since 9/11, the number of international students enrolled in U.S. institutions of higher learning has plummeted, and it will take a concerted effort on the part of education, business, and government to reverse the trend.

Foreign students who historically considered the United States for secondary or post secondary education are looking to new sources. Many now go to Australia, New Zealand, France, the United Kingdom, Germany, or the new virtual universities in India, Asia, and developing countries. The world's largest universities, with more than 100,000 students, have experienced dramatic growth through technology-based

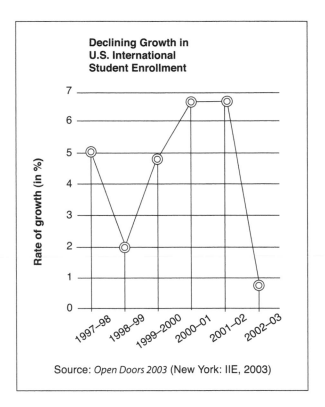

**Declining Growth in U.S. International Student Enrollment**

Rate of growth (in %)

1997–98  1998–99  1999–2000  2000–01  2001–02  2002–03

Source: *Open Doors 2003* (New York: IIE, 2003)

distance learning. Is this the answer for organizations in need of Q-Talent—developing nations developing your talent?

Here is a list of the largest universities in the world according to Wikipedia.com:

- Allama Iqbal Open University (Pakistan)
- Anadolu University (Turkey)
- Bangladesh Open University (Bangladesh)
- China Central Radio and TV University (China)
- Indira Ghandi National Open University (India)
- Indonesian Online Learning Unit (Indonesia)
- Korea National Open University (S. Korea)

- Payame Noor University (Iran)

- Sukothai Thammathirat Open University (Thailand)

Surprised? Have you approved any expense reports from your college recruiting team to these locations?

The number of natural science and engineering graduates has dramatically increased in some countries while remaining flat in the United States. From 1989 to 1990, China increased the number of B.A. grads in natural science and engineering by 150 percent, to 322,000. Mexico increased the number of M.A. and Ph.D. graduates in the sciences and engineering from 340 to 63,000 over the same time period. The United States experienced a small increase and, in 1999, graduated 77,000 M.A.s and Ph.D.s in natural science and engineering. Today, 1.6 percent of 24 year olds in the United States have a Bachelor's degree in engineering, whereas in Russia it is closer to 3.5 percent, and in China it is almost 5 percent. Which country is better prepared for the future?

Consider the implications that tightened U.S. immigration has had on one field of considerable strategic importance: physics. According to a June 2003 report from the American Institute of Physics (AIP), the percentage of foreign-born students enrolling in U.S. graduate physics programs declined dramatically after the 9/11 attacks. After steady increases for decades, enrollment in U.S. graduate physics programs declined 10 percent from 2001 to 2003. Two thirds of physics Ph.D. departments and half of all physics Master's programs reported that they had accepted students who were unable to attend because they could not secure visas.

As this example and the data preceding it illustrate, decreased foreign student enrollment in U.S. schools has several cascading effects that ultimately impact talent markets worldwide. Number one, of course, is that U.S. universities are now producing fewer scholars. One could also reasonably presume that the students denied entry across disciplines are more qualified academically than those who end up taking their places because the locked-out students were accepted over them in the first place. Third, universities have had a harder time filling their teaching assistant positions, which typically go to first-year graduate students. Yet another effect, noted earlier, is that the students denied entry will most likely end up being educated in their home country or other countries, and a significant portion of them will stay there, denying the U.S. labor market—and economy—needed Q-Talent.

All of us have to be thinking ahead about where our next generation of Q-Talent will come from. In the United States and some other countries, businesses are already clamoring for lawmakers to streamline immigration processes, either by hiring more customs and immigration officials, easing regulations, or simply increasing quotas to allow more students and business professionals. But with the high priority placed on security, it might be a long time before we see the ease of immigration, especially in the United States, that existed for centuries prior to September 11.

Whereas most people think that talent follows business, the reverse is happening as well. Businesses follow talent, too. A global pool of skilled workers is drawing companies that want to find Q-Talent, cut costs, and increase local sales. Which countries will benefit from this trend?

For example, Accenture has hired more than 2,000 people in the Philippines to do accounting, software, and back-office work; GE has hired 29,000 in India and China for finance, R&D, and IT support. GE was well ahead of this curve and not only hired and established business in India, they developed such a state-of-the-art support center in India that they have now spun off that business to become a profit center and offer their learning and business services to other corporations. Airlines, insurance, technology, and medical processing firms are all relocating to where the talent is to ensure they have access to right talent when they need it.

Relocations by individuals and companies and acquisitions add even more complexity to the mix. When companies relocate, they bring some talent from their country of origin, too. The best and brightest within the United States could decide that they must be in China or India to be where the action is and end up working for Chinese and Indian companies, not U.S. companies that happen to do business there. We will likely see more and more acquisitions of U.S.-based businesses by Chinese and Indian corporations, à la the IBM Personal

Computer acquisition. At engineering career fairs at Purdue, the University of Texas, and many other schools, your college recruiters are likely to be surrounded by booths from Legend Computers (China), Samsung (Korea), Nokia (Sweden), Sony (Japan), and other non-U.S. firms interested in hiring U.S. talent.

- What does tightened immigration mean for U.S. companies who have historically counted on foreign talent to fill in for domestic talent shortages or provide highly specialized skills?

- How will tightened U.S. immigration affect organizations worldwide?

- How will the talent market worldwide be affected by the surging economic opportunities in the countries—increasingly outside of the United States—where students remain after graduation?

## Offshoring

Another major trend affecting the talent market results from the plain old cost of labor. "Offshoring," the practice of moving jobs from industrialized nations to countries where wages and worker demands are less expensive, is the *en vogue* answer to the cost-of-labor challenge. Offshoring reflects a fundamental shift in the economies of developed nations—from manufacturing and production to service, management, and other "knowledge" work—while developing nations move into the relative prosperity of a manufacturing economy. Many so-called commoditized jobs—those that can be performed just about anywhere by people with the right skills and training—have been and will continue to be relocated.

In Vietnam, for example, the furniture industry has become large and lucrative, with companies such as Singapore's Koda Woodcraft and U.S.-based L&J.G. Stickley opening plants, along with many other companies from China, the United States, and elsewhere.

Although there is little doubt that relocating companies to Vietnam has cost jobs in these companies' home countries, there is also little doubt that impoverished Vietnam needs the economic boost this industry has provided. In Vietnam's developing economy, a furniture maker can eventually enjoy all the prestige and comfort that comes with earning a solid, upper-middle-class income.

Offshoring may become a given as the global economy slowly matures. In fact, many economists and business leaders argue that this decades-old practice has always been a given, that capitalism acts upon companies like nature acts upon animal species, forcing them to adapt and find the path of least resistance to survive. According to *The Wall Street Journal*, economists examined employment trends in 20 large economies around the globe and found that between 1995 and 2002, 22 million factory jobs had gone by the wayside. Contrary to popular American sentiment, the jobs did not disappear only in the United States. While the United States lost about 11 percent of its manufacturing jobs in that period, Japan lost 16 percent. Even developing nations lost factory jobs: Brazil suffered a 20 percent decline. China lost 15 percent. No country is immune. Furthermore, many companies are deciding to locate new product lines or other strategic initiatives outside of their own borders from the start, creating a huge, and largely hidden, talent shift.

Some say that offshoring allows the company to sell its product into the foreign market where it sets up shop, generating revenue and lowering costs for investors in the company's homeland; the revenue gains can, in turn, be reinvested, creating more jobs in the home country that are higher up the economic food chain. Others argue that relocating a call center to India provides little return other than some increased profits due to cost savings. Some folks in parts of Asia, Africa, Latin America, and elsewhere argue that offshoring is really *inshoring*, and is profoundly good for their local economies. Still others say that those local economies suffer as some companies seek to shirk the enforced labor standards of their home countries. Incidentally, inshoring to the United States also occurs. Today, more than 6.5 million Americans work for foreign companies with operations in the United States.[2]

---

[2] Source: Department of Commerce.

Regardless of where you stand on this issue, one thing is certain: It is not going away any time soon. Offshoring is powered by the same unstoppable, evolutionary economic forces that have pushed so many people off of the farm in Europe and North America for the past two centuries.

How does offshoring affect talent? Although, in the short term, job loss occurs when certain functions—or entire companies—move overseas, the changing demographics previously discussed will most likely take some of the heat off this sensitive issue in the longer term. With some predicting a shortage of workers in industrialized nations and with falling populations in developed nations worldwide, many experts believe that unemployment is likely to fall dramatically, creating a huge demand for more Q-Talent. Additionally, industry sectors, such as transportation, the professions, the service industry, and the financial industry, are all expected to grow by 15 percent or more, adding millions of jobs. Even production jobs are expected to grow, especially in the technology sector, albeit more modestly.

In some cases, offshoring means greater availability of talent due to technology. When a company moves some or all of its operations abroad, not only does the company have access to talent in the new market, they can still hire talent from their "home" market, or any other market for that matter, and work with them remotely. Whatever your feelings about offshoring, immigration, and the "global economy," it is hard to deny that the world has gotten just a little bit smaller, or as Friedman says, a little bit flatter. Just as today's technology has enabled some new forms of job exports, such as hospitals sending X-rays and CAT scans to radiologists overseas, it also has the power to extend the reach of any organization—and any person as well.

Today, a law firm in Hong Kong can hire a graphic designer in Seattle, Buenos Aries, or Auckland. It does not take a visa, a transcontinental flight, or a mountain of paperwork to get quality help from just about anywhere. As such, whether they know it or not, every business with a Web site is global. Whether your company is a major manufacturer of after-market auto parts or a small consultancy, your Web site can be seen and interacted with by anyone, anywhere. Many companies admit as much today: "We can hire you if you want to telecommute from Canada, but not if you want to relocate here in Germany."

Finally, offshoring is not always a slam dunk, and with it, companies risk creating more talent-related problems that they solve. Dell Computer Corp., the famous reseller of PCs, was forced to bring back some of its offshore customer service operations because of concerns over the quality of those services. In addition, many developing countries have a dire lack of qualified managers. The cost of relocating managers overseas can be prohibitively expensive, and the combination of these factors adds that much more complexity to the offshoring equation.

Offshoring represents another force in the business world that companies—and individuals—must confront. For our purposes, whether you are a British company hiring assembly line talent in China, a French company hiring sales representatives in the Middle East, a Chinese company hiring furniture makers in Vietnam, or a company that hires all of its employees domestically, the principles are the same: Q-Talent is always hard to find. You need Q-Talent at every level of your business to succeed. And the better prepared and informed you are, the better your technology, processes, and philosophy with regard to hiring the best talent, the better off you'll be.

- How does offshoring affect your industry?

- How will offshoring change your access to talent?

- What can you do to prepare for these changes and stay one step ahead of them?

## Emerging Talent Markets

Due in part to the trends described previously—a shrinking talent force in some countries, more restrictive U.S. immigration policies, and continued offshoring—emerging talent markets are forming in both developing countries and more mature economies, bringing with them new challenges and opportunities.

Developing nations are going through the same familiar shift toward industrialization that more mature economies saw a century ago. As manufacturing and other jobs migrate into new, developing regions, they create more wealth, more consumers, and more participants in the global economy.

We can already see results from recent industrialization, as poverty levels in some parts of the world have decreased. According to the World Bank Group's poverty monitoring home page, which provides estimates based on the best available survey data, the East Asia/Pacific region has seen a steady decline over the past decades in the number of people living on less than $1 a day (calculated by the World Bank at 1993 value), a commonly accepted measurement of extreme poverty. By this measurement, the region has gone from an estimated 57.7 percent poverty level in 1981, to 24.9 percent in 1993, to 14.9 percent in 2001. China alone has gone from 63.8 to 16.6 percent over the same period, which translates to 422 million fewer people living on less than $1 per day.

More than reducing the number of its poorest citizens, China is becoming more prosperous overall, emerging as the next true economic superpower. With that status has come more and more chances for its citizens to find work and new opportunities. Stories abound about young adults from rural areas leaving their small country farms for jobs in China's urban centers. As reported by Leslie T. Chang for *The Wall Street Journal,* estimates show that as many as 114 million people have participated in this migration, the largest "migrant" talent force in history.

Their experiences, both good and bad, will help shape the future of the Chinese economy, itself a cornerstone for the world's economic fortunes. Many of these migrant workers are finding jobs in ways that are reminiscent of the loading wharfs at seaboard cities in early-twentieth-century America—show up, line up, put your hand up. With factory floor jobs especially, often the first to raise a hand and display the willingness and the ability to do the work gets the job.

To help workers and companies connect, huge open-air talent markets have emerged in industrial cities such as Zhingtou, where factories find talent to fill positions of all types. At these talent "bazaars," recruiters hawk different factory jobs as workers walk by. The prospective worker is told of the factory, the work, and the pride and money that he will be able to send home.

Conditions at many of these factories are wholly unacceptable by Western standards. Factory floor workers might put in long hours. They might sleep in factory dormitories with up to a dozen co-workers.

They might work for low pay, often in dangerous conditions. Still, many find it difficult to leave their jobs because of the lack of a viable future in the rural villages they came from and the more enjoyable social life they find in the city.

These privations, too, resemble the America of a century ago. And so does the fact that, slowly, workers in China are beginning to understand their value and worth, that they are the country's greatest resource. Unlike the West's industrial revolution, this Asian economic renaissance has technology putting wind to the sails. Recruiting and retention will evolve rapidly there, too, free of the restrictions imposed by tradition.

For now, working conditions in China have a long way to go. But the fact that a young person can do something different, live away from the farm, find new friends and a new life, is exciting for many young people in China. This excitement has created unprecedented talent force energy for the country.

- How will the talent markets in China and other countries undergoing industrialization evolve as their economies mature and workers become savvier?

- How will the open-air talent market of Zhingtou influence the way that talent relationships are developed through technology?

- How will these changes affect China's global market position?

- What affect will these developments have on the rest of the world's economies and talent markets?

Meanwhile, more developed nations and regions are seeing new talent markets emerge as traditional factory and manufacturing jobs migrate elsewhere and technology, information, management, and service industries grow. Just as tractors made farming more efficient and reduced the demand for agricultural workers, technology has increased efficiency and reduced demand for certain types of jobs. In addition, technology has increased opportunities to contribute to growing industries in new ways and increased the demand for certain skills, such as managing, supporting, and analyzing technology-based processes. Where metropolitan areas once held the nerve center for a company's suburban and rural factory operations, industrialized nations now house the nerve centers for operations around the world.

As these economies evolve, most new jobs will require a college education, especially in medicine, accounting, engineering, and management.

- Where will companies find the next generation of Q-Talent to populate these industries?

There's another side to the emerging talent markets in developed nations. Many of the young workers in North America, Europe, and parts of Asia are acquiring more education and taking "knowledge worker" jobs rather than lining up to drive trucks, buses, or combines. Fewer young people want to work on the factory floor. But goods still have to be produced and transported. Crops still have to be harvested.

- Where will developed countries find this crucial hands-on talent?

# Recruiting-Specific Trends

In addition to the trends described so far in this chapter, there are two important trends to consider in the recruiting arena: recruitment process outsourcing and measuring talent, as discussed in the following subsections.

## Recruitment Process Outsourcing (RPO)

Recruitment process outsourcing (RPO), also called human resource outsourcing, is a subset of business process outsourcing (BPO), a move to outsource certain business functions. RPOs are a growing global industry designed to provide companies with the right talent at the right time. RPO takes the process over for you. According to Gartner, BPO revenues touched $46 billion in 2003, an 18 percent increase from 2002 revenue of $39 billion. Human resource BPO is forecasted to represent 39 percent of all BPO revenue in 2004—or around $20 billion.

The BPO segment is projected to be a $148 billion industry by 2008 (Forrester); human resource outsourcing is expected to retain a 20 percent share of that market.

What is the impact of RPO? It makes acquiring great talent that much more complex. The middlemen see the opportunity and will be there first to provide the talent-related solutions that seem too hard to figure out without them. A precursor to RPO happened years ago with the advent of temporary service companies, such as Kelly Services and Manpower. We have all used them at one point or another. We have all run the cost analysis a million times and gone back and forth as to whether this approach saves us money. We have all said we wished we did not have to have a third party between us and the people we depend on to run and build our businesses. We all have acquiesced to using a third party more than once in the face of formidable staffing needs. Any of this sound familiar? It is why leaders need to be thinking about and readying themselves now for the trends that affect their talent requirements. The next chapter discusses RPO at greater length.

## Measuring Talent

How can businesses measure whether their employees are properly aligned with their business goals and contributing to the success of the organization? Talent management and prediction products and services are beginning to help companies better understand their current and future talent needs. Managers are learning how to better understand their employees while companies are putting an emphasis on career paths to develop and retain their Q-Talent.

Companies need to do more to adopt the same rigors and disciplines in their talent practices as they have in areas such as inventory management. Whole industries and careers have been built on improving supply chain methods and results. The "talent supply chain" methods have yet to be defined and given the same level of criticality that is given to other parts of the business, such as identifying and sourcing raw materials. We like to measure what is important. What is more vital and core to your business than your talent? Chapter 6, "Tangible Talent Measurement," examines talent measurement in more detail.

**Where Have All the Young Scientists Gone?**

Bill Gates, chairman of Microsoft Corporation, knows who his real competition is. It is not SAP, Oracle, or IBM. It is Goldman Sachs and Lehman Brothers. For a variety of reasons, companies across the science and technology realm are vying for an ever-dwindling pool of young, bright engineers, programmers, doctors, biologists, and chemists. After years of mediocrity in space exploration, after the dot-com bust, after layoffs in defense and medicine during the 1990s, after years of job losses in high technology due to offshoring, and after decades of educational cutbacks, more and more kids are looking outside of the sciences when deciding on a career path. That is why Gates hit the road in 2004, stumping about the opportunities provided by careers in science and technology.

For many companies focused on science, technology, and medicine, the skills gap of the future is happening now, and Gates is not the only executive speaking out about it. In the U.S. defense industry alone, it is estimated that more than half of the talent base will retire by the mid-2020s. With the country's relatively ineffective education system (the United States spends about as much as any country on education, but its students routinely rank near the bottom in math and science), there is not much hope for a pipeline of talented young students to replace all those retirees any time soon. Therefore, jobs in the United States for science and engineering graduates will likely outpace the supply by a three-to-one margin as we move deeper into the twenty-first century.

Additionally, a number of factors exacerbate this situation. For one, the United States is now investing heavily in its national defense again. So, after nearly a decade of rolling back the headcount, the industry is being forced to ramp up. Only now, all of those people who would have been progressing into leadership positions over the past decade are not there. Where there should be a large pool of workers with 6 to 15 years of experience, there is only a big hole. This example is not merely an issue of corporate competition. It is a matter of national defense.

Another challenge facing this unique industry is that it cannot rely on immigration, or offshoring, to solve its talent conundrum. Only U.S. citizens can obtain the security clearance necessary for the industry's most sensitive projects. Add to this the fact that the U.S. Department of Homeland Security is requiring an integrated approach to its defense platforms, involving companies such as Accenture, CSC, and Booz Allen—systems integrators and consultants—who also introduce competition in the industry for the same talent.

Add it all up, and companies in the U.S. defense industry are facing what industry veterans might call "a situation." As of summer 2004, defense contractor Raytheon alone was looking to hire 6,000 people in the span of a year. How could it accomplish such a feat?

For Raytheon and others, this challenge is being met by an internal talent organization dedicated to recruiting the best and the brightest. Raytheon recruits at 140 schools across the United States, with 26 of those designated as "strategic universities." The company is working to develop strong, long-term relationships with these strategic schools. It sends senior management and top executives, often a vice president or even the CEO, to college campuses to talk to kids as early as freshman orientation. The company is even considering permanent offices on some campuses to build those relationships over time.

Those are sound principles for the long term, but the company's short-term hiring picture is more urgent. For Raytheon, it may take a talent-oriented merger or acquisition to get the necessary amount of "clear talent"—people with security clearances that can step in and contribute right away. In this scenario, there may not be any value from a financial or product standpoint to justify the acquisition. It is the talent that would make such a deal attractive.

This is an example of what can happen in the arena of talent when socio-economic forces collide. The only way for any company to get ahead of this kind of challenge is to dedicate their best and smartest people to the problem and take a strategic, proactive approach. A company without the right people and processes in place could easily find itself overwhelmed by a situation, such as the one facing Raytheon and other U.S. defense contractors.

If this kind of "perfect storm" of talent issues suddenly hit your industry, would your company be ahead of the game, or struggling to catch up? Which company is going to win when that happens? There will be at least one winner in every competitive industry or market segment. The question is, who will it be?

## The Demand for a New Approach

The trends presented in this chapter require businesses that "get it" to rethink the way talent is assessed, recruited, trained, retained, and promoted. In this new environment, the "arrogance of supply"—disregard for the importance of great talent that some companies have grown accustomed to through decades of labor abundance—will become more the exception than the rule. In a complicated, global, high-tech economy, many of the old assumptions about how to attract good people, fill positions, and nab Q-Talent when it is available no longer apply.

As with any major shift, companies that prepare and adapt will succeed, and those that do not will be challenged to survive. Without great people, how do you grow? You do not. Without great people, how do you bring new products, technologies, and services to the marketplace? You do not. It is not just about executives. It is not just about the United States, or Germany, or Japan. It is about every organization in every country in this gigantic greenhouse called Earth.

Companies do not allow gaps in their financial projections, business plans, or supply chains. They do not tolerate inefficiencies in their schedules, quality control measures, or production lines. So why do companies permit talent gaps and other recruiting inefficiencies? Why are they continually caught unaware by open positions, responding—again and again—by scrambling around like a farmhouse hen? If companies want to be the best they can be, they can no longer approach recruiting in the same old way.

Already, forward-thinking organizations are changing—gaining awareness of trends, reacting to new realities, and preparing for future developments. Global competition for Q-Talent is beginning to heat up, and certain companies are beginning to take a long-term, competitive view of their talent equation. Throughout this book, we show you some of the strategic, creative ways that these companies are getting ahead of the competition by finding and hiring Q-Talent.

Q-Talent is scarce, but it feels much scarcer if you are not doing anything about it. When the trends outlined here begin to accelerate, the traditional, reactive, "where's-the-approved-job-requisition" method of hiring—where you do not even begin to think about looking for qualified candidates until a position becomes open—will create serious problems for companies still mired in this approach. These companies will scramble to catch up, believing they can make it work like it always has; but this time, competitors will have thought ahead, and the scrambling company will feel the effects of its competitor's advantage.

If you have ever run a marathon, or know someone who has, you know that training is critical. With the right training regime, started early enough, running a marathon is a manageable challenge. On the other hand, insufficient training leads to potentially dire consequences on race day. For those who start their marathon training too late, it will be next to impossible to best the competition.

Prepare now, or suffer the consequences later. Much more than a laundry list of problems and challenges, the trends outlined in this chapter represent an extraordinary opportunity for companies that plan ahead and work toward the future, starting today.

In the next chapter and beyond, we help you start to make this vision a reality by developing long-term goals and adopting a more strategic and targeted approach to attract and retain top talent. The first step, covered in Chapter 3, "Building a Competitive Talent Organization," is to establish a focused talent organization led by a savvy "Chief Talent Officer."

# 3

# BUILDING A COMPETITIVE TALENT ORGANIZATION

---

*Forces in Play:* Companies develop their strategic recruiting capabilities. A new type of recruiter emerges at the executive and operational levels. This role becomes a critical component of any competitive business.

---

The goal of recruiters and the organizations they work for is to have Q-Talent ready for current *and* future opportunities—a steady flow of the right people, ahead of the company's demand for them. Picture an airport with airplanes circling overhead. The talent organization is the control tower. It needs to know who is on the horizon, what their skills are, and whether the company has an empty runway available to bring them in for a landing.

The traditional, reactive human resources organization of the past is a major liability for companies going forward. Focusing on HR compliance, filling open positions, and waiting around for the next position to open up and then throwing "warm bodies" at it will no longer suffice for organizations that want to remain competitive in a talent-scarce market. Asking a product manager, who is already working 70 hours a week, to spend 10 more hours screening candidates or even reviewing resumés, just will not do anymore.

The fact is, most hiring decisions in corporations are made by middle- and upper-management. HR may help facilitate the process, mining for resumés and such, but usually in a reactive mode by responding to a new job requisition, without centralized coordination and strategy. Therefore, great talent slips through the cracks. Candidates find themselves rejected for jobs that do not quite fit, when ones that do are right around the corner. They are told there are no opportunities, even though an impending retirement is about to create one or a new company initiative is about to create several. They are put off by bad Web copy or a lack of responsiveness.

In each case, a more informed, proactive recruiting organization could have headed off the problem and turned it into an opportunity. But most companies do not spring into action until after an impending talent crisis has been identified. And then . . . they start "planning."

At this point, it is too late to start planning. By then, you must be in full-scale implementation to fix the crisis and fix it now. If the future of your business depends on your ability to find and develop great talent, why would you wait until you have to dig yourself out of a hole?

This chapter shows you how to create a strategic, proactive talent organization that will not only reduce the costs associated with recruiting great talent, but will build and return value to your company as well.

## Recruiting Models: A Look Back

Recruitment has been around a long time and has played an important role in building not just companies, but all kinds of organizations. Whether it is a head of state recruiting political allies, a sales organization wooing another company's top performer, or a sports team landing a desirable free agent, securing Q-Talent has long been imperative to the success of just about any organization.

In the 1990s, some industries, notably the technology industry, experienced rapid growth and correspondingly fierce competition for Q-Talent. To help meet this intense need, great recruiters commanded hefty salaries. Then, as we all know, the so-called dot-com bubble burst. As companies withered and dried up, the experienced talent from those companies became eager and available to work for the companies that remained. As competition for that talent decreased, so did the need for internal strategic recruiters who intimately knew the business, the market, and how to successfully recruit the right Q-Talent for the company.

Many of those highly paid recruiters were let go, and the responsibility for filling the company's talent needs fell mainly into the hands of generalist HR representatives. This cost-cutting move seems sensible on the surface. However, it usually leaves the company unable to effectively and proactively achieve its talent objectives.

HR generalists typically spend time on everything from payroll and benefits administration to corrective actions to employee orientation. They are often inundated with mountains of paperwork. As a result, they have little time to develop their understanding of the business, its vision, its strategy, and the competitive landscape. Furthermore, some HR organizations do not have adequate credibility with management to begin with and therefore are not looked to as a strategic partner for the business. They do not have the ear of the king, so to speak. All of these factors present a big struggle for the recruiting profession.

Another effect of passing the recruiting buck to overworked generalists is that when it comes time to hire, they are forced to react because they have not been spending time lining up great talent to plug into future opportunities. They do not have candidates ready who have been screened and are interested in the company. So they search a stagnant database hoping to find a relatively recent resumé. They place an ad in the newspaper or on a public job board. They jump into full recruitment mode after weeks of not thinking about it.

To some extent, companies can get by with this reactive approach as long as the talent for their industry is abundant. It is not ideal, but it works. HR generalists typically cost less than half as much as the recruiters of a decade ago. So, until companies see revenue losses as a result of not securing the right talent, this less expensive talent model will persist in many organizations.

However, as previously discussed, talent scarcity will become a reality for many industries. To prepare, many forward-thinking companies are already developing innovative recruiting practices, and this trend will only increase. In addition, as you will see, companies stand to gain real, bottom-line benefits from creating an effective talent organization.

## Emerging Recruitment Practices

What is happening in the recruitment field today? Recruitment varies by region. In the East, recruiting is just beginning to emerge as a discipline. Relatively free of tradition in this area, Asia is becoming a land of innovative recruiting, as evidenced by open talent markets, such as the one in Zhingtou described in Chapter 2, "Talent Market Demands." Economic growth in any environment depends on the ability to source, attract, recruit, and deploy the right talent at the right time in the right place. With economies in Asia expanding, talent will become an increasingly important factor, and the recruiting industry will respond with new recruiting skills and models.

In the West, including Europe, the recruiting industry is evolving and finding new ways to align its business models with those of the companies it serves. One model gaining traction in these regions is the recruitment process outsourcer (RPO) introduced in Chapter 2, where a recruiting agency takes on all recruitment activities for a client company. This model has been around for a long time. In Europe, the recruitment consultancy, or agency, has played a prominent role in the recruitment process. Almost all positions at all levels are turned over to an agency to fill. But Europe's recruiters are not always innovative in their approach. Many agencies still rely solely on newspaper and Internet ads to attract the appropriate talent. And their business model is based on a fee, generally calculated as a percentage of a hired candidate's first year salary, which is an expensive model for companies to support.

RPOs became better known more recently in the European market when Bank of America outsourced all of its recruitment activities with the goals of reducing redundancies and lowering costs. The bank's outsourcer, Exult, agreed to a large contract with razor-tight margins. Exult has achieved profitability with this model, and other companies, such as Convergys, have also had success with it and legitimized this model as a strategy to help companies reduce costs. This practice will likely play an important role in recruiting efforts of the future, although industry insiders argue as to exactly how or to what degree.

Although the value proposition for this model is based on lowering cost, in a more competitive market, lowering costs is not enough. In the future, especially in industries facing a dearth of talent, the value proposition will shift to a recruiter's ability to deliver Q-Talent. To effectively deliver Q-Talent, a recruiter must have a deeper understanding of the business than most recruiters have today. At the same time, the candidates that companies are always looking for expect more today, because they know more—about your industry, your company, your market, and your competition. A recruiter who cannot answer a candidate's fundamental business questions will not have the credibility to secure Q-Talent, particularly top-level individuals.

Recruiters will also have to learn how to recruit Q-Talent from different cultures around the world. Understanding and accepting others' values will become a key requirement for the successful recruiter in our connected world that is getting smaller every day. Recruiters with the ability to source, attract, and deliver Q-Talent from any global locale will become necessary and vital components to any recruiting strategy. These recruiters will quickly become valued Q-Talent themselves and will be compensated accordingly.

Recruiters can deliver Q-Talent whether the recruiter is employed by the organization he is hiring for or whether he sits in an outside agency that works on behalf of the organization. Each type of recruiter can add value to clients by delivering on different value propositions through different business models. Internal recruiters are likely to have a better understanding of the organization and its needs and use this knowledge to make a strong case for candidates to work there. However, the volume of positions they are trying to fill can make it difficult for them to nurture one-on-one relationships with prospective Q-Talent.

External recruiters, or RPOs, might manage fewer openings and, as a result, have time to develop closer relationships with prospective talent. They are motivated to fill open positions because that is how they are paid. By representing multiple companies, external recruiters have more opportunities to offer prospective talent.

On the other hand, from the hiring organization's perspective, the RPO's breadth might lead them to place an ideal candidate at another company. Also, the RPO might lack the in-depth business understanding necessary to "close the deal." Finally, by working on behalf of your organization, external recruiters use your company's brand to build valuable talent relationships, assets that they—not your organization—own.

A successful mix of both models—internal recruiting organizations and strategic RPOs—will likely emerge. For positions where there is an abundance of talent, recruiters will take a more easily managed, "transactional" approach to filling these positions with the right people. For difficult-to-fill positions, such as those requiring highly specialized skills, RPOs might help an organization extend its reach to acquire the right candidates. Positions requiring Q-Talent will necessitate a more strategic approach by both internal recruiters and RPOs. Both approaches should be carefully managed by someone who understands each model and has been successful in both worlds.

**Guidelines for Global Recruiting**

The Internet has tied the world community more closely together. As a result, even small businesses might find themselves recruiting from pools of talent outside their nation's borders. For large companies, global recruiting is more relevant—and necessary—than ever to acquire the best talent.

When working with professionals abroad, be sensitive and understanding about their cultural heritage. Act with professionalism and grace as *they* define it. This applies to domestic recruiting as well, of course, but one's behavior may have pronounced consequences in other parts of the world. Although volumes could be written on this topic, the following are some basic points to get you started:

- Research the history and culture of the region—completely. Make sure you understand cultural expectations for interpersonal communications, body language, dining, and travel.

- Whether recruiting on the phone, the Internet, or in person, be aware that you are a guest and should act accordingly, with a high degree of neighborly graciousness.

- Extend your reach by using Internet technology to build relationships with a global community of Q-Talent ahead of actual demand.

- When talking with a prospect, give the person your complete concentration. Listen. In person, show the person you are paying attention, although strong eye contact might be considered impolite in some regions.

- Do not open your mouth to speak until the other party has completed his or her statement.

- Stick to business; do not make remarks regarding current events, politics, religion, and so on—no jokes.

- Thank your prospect at the end of the interview and clearly state your recruiting process.

- If the discussion requires follow up, then follow up promptly.

Internal recruiters and RPOs focus on hiring. A third approach is to outsource not only hiring, but also compensation, benefits, and overall management responsibilities for certain positions. Although it might be acceptable to outsource tactical positions, companies should not outsource positions that are key to their success. Companies that recognize the strategic value of Q-Talent will not outsource these positions.

While the recruiting industry continues to evolve, there will always be companies that view *all* of their talent as strategic Q-Talent and resist outsourcing the hiring and management of their most valuable asset. These are the organizations that will find themselves in a strong position to create lasting value from their recruitment and retention activities.

The recruiting industry will continue to face challenges as it strives to meet the talent needs of organizations worldwide. In the United States, one of the main challenges is keeping up with the demand for recruiters who have the full complement of skills needed to lead and deliver on a talent agenda. Europe is working to find and advance a new business model that protects the recruitment industry while helping client companies protect margins and compete globally. In China and the rest of Asia, the challenge is finding talent without the support of a traditional recruiting infrastructure.

## The Strategic Integration Point Person

As with any critical business function, such as finance, marketing, procurement, or operations, the only way to ensure success is to put someone competent in charge of it. Marketing, for example, cannot be run simply by managing daily tasks. Someone must own the creation of a strategy to support sales of the product or service. Typically, this person's success is tied to the amount of revenue derived from the strategic marketing initiatives put forth and possibly other metrics, such as customer retention and satisfaction.

To this end, your company needs to have a strategic integration point person for its talent objectives—a Chief Talent Officer—to ensure that the talent organization is empowered with the responsibility, knowledge, and tools to add strategic value to the business and achieve bottom-line results. If your company does not have the right person in charge of talent, then, by default, it does not have a process in place to acquire talent or measure how talent is affecting the business. A company without someone in charge of talent might not even know what its talent needs are.

For a talent leader to be successful, she should . . .

- Hold an executive position.

- Be respected in the organization.

- Possess a strong business background.

- Have full support from the CEO.

- Have direct lines of communication with other department heads.

Some executives might look at this list and say that HR and recruiting can have a "seat at the table" when they earn it. But would you ever say that about your CFO? If you are a company leader and you respond this way, chances are you do not have anyone in your current HR organization who can operate at the necessary strategic business level. If this is the case, it is incumbent upon you to identify the right talent to lead your organization's recruiting efforts and put that person in place. If you are a CEO and you lack confidence in your HR department, this is an opportunity to correct that situation.

This represents an opportunity for other company leaders as well. If you are the company's current HR leader and lack strategic business skills, ask for development, put a plan in place, and stretch yourself. Your efforts to develop new skills on top of needed HR skills will enhance your career value. If you currently work in a function other than HR, consider applying your business skills to the talent organization—a new line of career development might await.

The talent leader needs enough stature and clout in the company to make things happen. In many companies, as mentioned previously, HR organizations are not perceived as bringing real strategic value to the business and, as a result, lack credibility and influence with other operating units. This dynamic, of course, has a major effect on the way HR is seen, heard, and perceived throughout the company.

The talent leader could have "dotted-line" responsibility and report to several top-level company directors, as is often the case for those in charge of a centralized group, such as investor relations. Or she could report directly to a senior executive. Again, for the talent leader to succeed, she requires direct access to senior leadership.

The talent leader's goal is to align the talent organization directly with the business both strategically and tactically so that it is a true partner that brings real insight to solving the company's talent challenges and improving the business overall. To achieve this, the talent leader needs to understand the business from top to bottom and know the company's strategy at the highest level, including where the company is going, how it plans to get there, and what its strengths and weaknesses are. This person must be able to combine that knowledge with an understanding of the skills and experience needed for each position and the importance of those positions to the business itself.

The talent leader needs to be able to "tell the company story" as thoroughly and as fluently as the chief marketing officer, the head of investor relations or public affairs, the chief financial officer, and the CEO. In fact, the talent leader might need to tell the story better than anyone else to bring Q-Talent to the table.

With the right talent leader in place at the right level, your company can begin to take a proactive approach to its talent needs. Suppose, for example, that the talent leader is in an executive meeting the first time you discuss expanding into Asia. With this knowledge, the talent leader can make sure that the talent organization responds appropriately.

Recruiters can begin to approach any current employees who speak Mandarin or other dialects of Chinese, along with Korean, Japanese, Hindi, Malay, and Thai, find out whether they might be interested in the opportunities that loom on the horizon, and initiate any training or relocation efforts that will need to take place. The talent organization can begin thinking about executives to lead the new office, research the business climate in the new market to identify local leaders, and build the necessary recruiting relationships. The talent organization will also keep an eye out for new candidates who possess skills, knowledge, or other ties to this new business need and consider bringing those individuals into the company with an eye toward the future. With only this single piece of strategic knowledge—that the company plans a move into Asia—the talent organization can begin thinking ahead and getting ahead.

When talent is established as a strategic imperative for the business, it becomes much easier for the head of talent to achieve this kind of business alignment. If talent is a priority for the business, senior leaders will make it a priority to communicate their talent objectives. In fact, consider holding other executives accountable for their contributions to the talent organization. If you are serious about acquiring and retaining Q-Talent, measure efforts related to it as you measure other important business metrics. Chapter 6, "Tangible Talent Measurement," discusses talent measurement at length. With proper engagement from the company's leadership, the head of talent will have a much clearer understanding of the business strategies and be able to more effectively turn those strategies into a compelling recruitment plan.

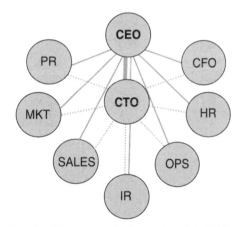

Much like the head of investor relations, the Chief Talent Officer must have a direct link to the CEO and every functional leader in order to understand the company's objectives and strategy and translate those into competitive talent initiatives.

# Clarian Health's Proactive Talent Organization

Clarian Health shows how a strategic talent leader can build a talent organization that has a positive impact on an organization's talent needs and its bottom line. In 2001, Clarian Health, a major medical system in Indiana with more than 11,000 employees, was facing a 16 percent vacancy rate and a 12.6 percent turnover rate in registered nurses. With a staff of about 3,100 RNs, that is a shortage of nearly 500 nurses, with nearly 400 more leaving each year.

Due to numerous slow points and hiccups in the process, the company's "hiring pipeline"—defined as the point at which initial contact with an applicant is made to the point at which he or she begins working—averaged a whopping 114 days. Also, because of the large vacancy rate, Clarian was spending $17 million annually on expensive "traveler nurses" who fly between regions, work defined contracts, and move on.

How did Clarian address the situation? Recognizing the need for leadership in this area, Senior Vice President Karlene Kerfoot took the first step and hired industry veteran and consultant Suellyn Ellerbe to help fix the troubled recruiting and retention functions, and ultimately all of the system's employment services. (If you are wondering, Ellerbe's title is head of the office of budget, finance, and resource management.) Experienced with just about every facet of hospital operations, Ellerbe brought a strong business sense and solid industry experience to Clarian's recruiting challenges.

Ellerbe and Kerfoot recognized immediately that Clarian's main challenge was not just to recruit a ton of nurses, but more importantly, to solve the problems that were creating the shortage in the first place. This meant looking at turnover issues and steps the company could take to develop and retain a workforce for the future.

Ellerbe began with the recruiting organization itself. The recruiting team had traditionally taken a passive approach. Nurse recruiters responded to applications or phone calls and placed about 90 percent of those applicants. Ellerbe could see that there was not much actual "recruiting" going on.

She decided to build a new culture around the talent function, with a strong marketing focus and a commitment to finding the best people for the organization. To start, she hired some people who shared her sensibilities. She trained the staff in sales techniques they could use to sell the organization and invested in the tools they would need to do so. She also installed leading-edge talent acquisition solutions, including candidate relationship and applicant-tracking technology from Hire.com, a firm founded and led by one of the authors, to support the recruiters in their jobs.

Clarian's new talent organization started by tackling their troubled hiring pipeline. They reengineered every segment of the process, bringing the hefty 114-day average down to 35 days. For staff nurses, their most critical need, the hiring pipeline now stands at just 14 days.

The team also looked at the hospital system's image campaign, holding focus groups with nurses in the community to determine the overall perception of Clarian in its market. Using the data from these focus groups, they conducted internal focus groups to decide how to go about marketing the nurses currently working at Clarian, and to help them craft messages about the organization's services. After that, Ellerbe's group engaged a firm to create an entirely new talent brand and corresponding campaign. The campaign's theme, "Be the nurse you have always wanted to be," was a resonant message that has proved successful.

The team also focused on Clarian's partnerships with various professional organizations, such as the American Association of Critical Care Nurses, Sigma Theta Tau International (the nursing honor society), the American Organization of Nurse Executives, the American Organization of Operating Room Nurses, the Black Nurses Association, the Filipino Nurses Association, and several others. The team not only attended these groups' events, but also created partnerships with them that featured joint projects or cooperation in areas of emphasis for each group. In this way, Clarian has almost become a part of the branding for the groups themselves. For example, the groups' brochures list Clarian, not as advertising, but as part of the work they do.

Finally, the group examined Clarian's events—job fairs, conferences, and its own open house events. The team worked to create a more professional, welcoming atmosphere at these events, where each potential candidate felt like he or she was welcomed and valued.

Amazingly, Ellerbe and her team laid all of this groundwork in a few months. By this time, they had created a solid foundation for Clarian's talent efforts. Since that time, they have worked to identify trends in the company's turnover figures and address them. They have created "retention specialists," new positions staffed by experienced nurses who focus on uncovering the real, human reasons behind nurse retention issues *and* fixing them.

As a result of all these proactive efforts, the company's vacancy rate has fallen from 16 percent to less than 5 percent. The turnover rate has dropped from nearly 13 percent to less than 7 percent and is still falling. What is more, due to the more efficient hiring pipeline and the new emphasis on service and excellence in the hiring process, the company's applicant dropout rate went from more than 15 percent to less than 1 percent.

Fewer positions open. Fewer opening up. Fewer applicants dropping out. A drastically shorter time to hire. With a $10,000 average cost for every hire, Clarian has realized a huge savings each year that directly affects the company's bottom line.

And what about the traveler nurses, the outside labor cost that was running about $17 million per year? In the first year after it implemented its recruiting changes, Clarian saved $10 million on traveling nurse costs by decreasing the nursing vacancy rate and thereby the need for traveler nurse services. Since then, they have continued to decrease their use of traveling nurses.

What is the value of creating a distinct talent organization and putting a great leader in charge of it? The answer will differ for each company, but there are success stories like Clarian's all around. Companies that take steps to get ahead of their talent needs by designating a "Chief Talent Officer" and creating a focused talent organization usually find surprising returns on the investment. In addition, the value they gain in terms of reputation and stature—reflected in the talent brand—will bring companies continuing intangible returns far into the future.

## New Recruiting Tools, Structures, and Processes

As the Clarian example illustrates, companies need a strong talent leader *and* a focused talent organization. Properly organized and run, a lean, proactive, competitive talent organization is not another business expense but rather an asset and a major way to build wealth in almost any organization.

The first thing companies must do in creating a talent organization is to recognize talent as the strategic priority that it is. Examine your HR organization. Figure out which functions relate to your talent objectives and which relate to administration, transactions, benefits, and compliance. Make sure the staff and resources dedicated to recruiting are separate from those dedicated to HR generalist functions. It is fine to locate your company's recruiting function in the general HR department *as long as* the recruiting and HR generalist functions are separate.

Whether recruiting remains in the overall HR organization or becomes a standalone business unit depends on your business and organizational models. The important part is to think of recruiting as a separate discipline and give it priority, visibility, accountability, and clout within the organization, so informed decisions about talent can be made and acted upon.

According to Mike Mayeux, founder and CEO of the recruiting firm Novotus, there are two "royal figures" in the recruitment process—the talent and the person seeking to hire that talent. The recruiter serves as an informational conduit, a concierge to that process who does his best to make it a good experience for everybody involved.

Sounds simple, but sheer numbers challenge the recruiter at every turn. Recruiters are outnumbered thousands to one on the candidate side and dozens to one on the hiring-manager side. The recruiter can only respond to folks on each end—whether candidate or hiring manager—one at a time. All the while, the companies' future profits, growth, teams, cultures, and initiatives hang in the balance. For the candidates, it is their careers.

The numbers that constantly challenge recruiters lead to some unfortunate consequences. People apply for jobs and nobody gets back to them. People talk to a recruiter once and never hear from them again. Applicants who are treated this way usually do not come back for more, leaving the recruiter in a constant search for new talent.

Cutting through the "noise" represents a huge opportunity for recruiters. But how can they do it? According to Mayeux, the key is the right framework through which to efficiently funnel candidates and organize the overall process. To that end, Novotus has developed an approach that combines technology and an innovative team, or "pod," recruiting structure. This approach enables them to reach out to thousands of candidates at a time, keep everyone informed, and keep the process moving.

As with any business unit, it is up to each company to create the structure and processes that make sense for them. The roles listed here can be located in separate groups or be part of an integrated department. A single individual might perform two or three of the roles.

A competitive recruiting organization should include these four major roles:

- **The recruiter.** This is the human, operational-level integration person who understands the company's story, the needs of each individual candidate and department, and how to use all of those factors to create compelling messages and other marketing tactics that "sell" the company's employment experience.

- **The administrator.** This is the classic support person who keeps tabs on everything, directs traffic, keeps track of names, appointments, and where each prospective candidate is in the recruiting process. This person might even monitor chat sessions and answer questions submitted via the company's employment Web site.

- **The technologist.** This is the person who can implement the company's employment messages online and build the Web solutions necessary to capture and build relationships with new talent.

- **The data analyst.** As discussed in the next chapter, recruiters perform some key marketing activities, such as capturing and analyzing data. Companies must understand their ideal demographics, craft messages to be as effective as possible, and continually measure results to fine-tune the efforts. The data analyst performs much the same function in recruiting as he would in the marketing department, helping ensure that the company is reaching the right candidates with the right messages.

Let's look at how Novotus uses these roles to recruit talent for its client companies. "Level II recruiters" are on the front lines. These highly experienced recruiters stay in a constant decision mode, deciding who goes where in the process. In most recruiting firms, these folks would be stuck in the time-consuming process of qualifying individuals and reviewing resumés that we described earlier, a losing proposition because of the overwhelming numbers involved.

At Novotus, the Level II recruiters are backed up by the technology and administrative professionals who keep the process moving. As a result, Level II recruiters are freed from most administrative tasks and busy-work. Instead, they are constantly in front of customers, talking to customers, figuring out what their needs are, and then sending them in the appropriate direction. Their job is to find candidates who match what the hiring manager is looking for, drive the process to a "short list" of Q-Talent candidates, and review the short list with the hiring manager.

Aside from the front-line, Level II recruiter, each talent service team has one person who is the administrator or team leader. This person, a Level I recruiter, keeps track of the job searches, knows who is working on what, and monitors the team's overall progress. They also run the communications console, live chat, live support, and respond to e-mail. They take incoming information and act on it by scheduling meetings, making phone calls, or doing any other necessary tasks to keep the process moving. They send out meeting and interview confirmations so that everybody knows where to go, what time to be there, how to dress, and any other pertinent information.

On the technology side, Novotus uses queued workflows and e-mail, employing rules and filters to ensure that the most important e-mails are visible quickly. There is also live support, and each team, or pod, includes a chat operator who answers questions that arise. The work-flow is designed so that each correspondence drives a person to the next logical step, so that the Level II recruiter can constantly serve multiple individuals.

According to Mayeux, the advantages of a team of specialists are that everybody stays focused, works more efficiently, and uses his or her skills and experience to the greatest extent possible.

For the company that needs Q-Talent, this structure offers three main benefits: better, faster, and cheaper. Better quality candidates, and better, more personalized communication with the recruiter. A faster process overall. And as a result, greater cost efficiency throughout the process.

Need proof? Consider the following request, which would approach ridiculous in most recruiting environments.

A Fortune 500 company, seeking to open a call center in Latin America, needed to hire 80 managers in 3 weeks and then add 450 call center workers in another 3 to 4 weeks. Furthermore, there was not a single candidate to begin with. Nobody.

In the first 9 days, between 6,000 and 8,000 people visited the Novotus Web site talent community for that market. Novotus scheduled 220 interviews, filling the docket for a dozen hiring managers. The following week, they did another 220 interviews. The company was able to hire its 80 managers in 3 weeks, on schedule. Moving on to the call center workers, Novotus collaborated with a government entity to drive solid candidates into the interview process. Ultimately, 550 people were hired in about 7 weeks.

Where did all this talent come from and how did Novotus respond so quickly? At the time, the region had high unemployment and a highly educated talent pool. The government and client heavily promoted the job openings and included Novotus's URL on billboards and in relevant interviews and news articles. On their end, Novotus had carefully engineered their workflow to prepare for a high volume of candidates and leaned on technology to accelerate the process. For example, they created a customized intranet site for scheduling and other tasks.

As a result of their preparation and infrastructure, Novotus's results were accomplished by one Level II recruiter, supported by Novotus's Internet-based technology and team concept. As testament to the technology, Level I recruiters were chatting online with 10 to 12 applicants at a time throughout the process. Imagine how many recruiters—and how long, and how much money—it would take to work through that many candidates by telephone.[1]

---

[1] Note: The technology in this example is provided by Hire.com, the company where one of the book's authors is founder and president.

According to Mayeux, this process is not limited to reactive, mass-hire situations. It is effective for huge projects as well as for individual searches. The company routinely fills positions for CFOs, controllers, lead programmers, and more. In one instance, Mayeux himself met a client on a plane trip, a CEO needing to hire a new controller. At the next layover, Mayeux contacted Novotus. By the end of the next flight, Novotus had delivered four solid candidates, plus a couple more that Mayeux knew off the top of his head.

"We'll introduce you to the person that you're going to hire in the first three to five days of your search," says Mayeux. "That would be impossible if we didn't have the right people, working in the team environment, supported by excellent processes and technology."

## Creating Your Talent Plan

Now that you have created a distinct talent organization and the talent leader has aligned the group with the organization's business goals, it is time for the talent leader and his team to create a talent plan.

A comprehensive talent plan delineates the company's recruiting and deployment strategies by business unit and by position within each unit. Additionally, the talent plan includes measurable forecasts, such as recruitment and deployment costs, time to acquisition, and time to productivity for new talent. The talent plan allows the talent leader and other executives, including the CEO, to manage and measure this function alongside the rest of the business.

To build an effective talent plan, the talent organization needs to understand the following broad areas that are key to the company's success:

- The company's goals and objectives
- Key milestones that must be accomplished to meet those goals and objectives
- The problem that the company's goods or services solve, or the needs they fill in the marketplace
- The size of the problem or need, and the value of solving or filling it

- Special or unique aspects of the company's products, solutions, or approach

- The customer who uses those goods or services, and how the goods or services are used

- What it takes to build, sell, deploy, and maintain the company's products or services

- The company's distribution and supply models, including key industry partners and their core skills

- The company's competitors, their offerings, and how the company strives to differentiate itself from the competition

A lot of this information should reside in the company's business plan. The talent organization can acquire the rest of it by reaching out to the company's leaders.

Together, these pieces of information form a story about the company and where it is going. After the talent organization understands these factors, they must stay in tune with them as the business continues to evolve. With access to the company's senior leadership, the talent leader is properly positioned to funnel information about strategic business issues to the talent organization.

With this broad understanding of the organization in hand, the talent organization then needs to approach department leaders and hiring managers to tie those high-level business goals to specific talent needs at the departmental level. People from the talent organization should ask departmental leaders and hiring managers for the following information to complete the overall talent plan:

- How the department aligns with and supports the overall business

- What the departmental goals are and how progress is measured against those goals

- An outline of the critical skills and positions necessary for the department to be successful, and how those skills and positions help the company accomplish its strategic goals

- Examples of ideal Q-Talent candidates, including specific qualification parameters

- Departmental initiatives, projects, or other activities that may affect talent needs, including any expected launch dates, release-to-manufacturing dates, or other corporate deadlines that must be factored into hiring decisions

The talent organization should use this information to make sure the talent plan includes expected talent needs by department, along with a rationale for why those positions are important for the business and their potential impact on the bottom line. For each critical position and skill set, the talent plan should outline core competencies, qualification parameters, and examples of the ideal kind of Q-Talent. The plan should discuss these positions in light of department or project goals, and how those departments or projects align with overall corporate strategy.

Just as the overall business goals change, departmental initiatives and projects are in constant motion. Therefore, the talent organization must stay in frequent contact with departmental leaders and hiring managers to find out what is changing and how it impacts the groups' talent needs. This relationship works in reverse, too: Department heads and hiring managers must keep their contacts in the talent organization in the loop on issues that may affect hiring needs. The talent organization links the "troops" on the ground and the "generals" back at the command center. Open lines of communication ensure that recruitment efforts align with the company's strategic objectives.

## Aligning with Marketing

No talent plan is complete without a set of compelling messages that the company can apply to its recruitment efforts across all communication channels—in person, in the media, and in cyberspace. Traditionally, individual recruiters generate these messages with little organizational rigor or control over what messages are used, and with little cooperation between recruiters and the hiring managers they represent.

The best way to understand the importance of recruitment messaging is to analyze most companies' efforts to market their products and services.

It is hard to imagine a successful company that does not have some kind of marketing—skilled people working to position a company's products or services in the marketplace with compelling messages to help drive sales. Marketers not only create and coordinate these messages, they also report on which visuals and messages work with target audiences and continually improve any messages that are not hitting the "sweet spot."

The next chapter discusses "talent brands," how they differ from the product brand, and some ideas to help you create a compelling set of talent brand messages. To create a talent brand, your new talent organization must be strongly aligned with your marketing organization.

Each is a valuable asset for the other. With close cooperation between the company's marketing and recruiting efforts and the messages each uses, the talent brand and the product brand can support and even enhance one another's objectives. Companies without this connection are missing a key piece to ensuring that their new talent efforts return the most value to the company.

The talent organization can begin to lay the groundwork for this new employment-marketing effort when it obtains information from departments and hiring managers during creation of the talent plan. Obtain the following information from department leaders to help you develop appropriate, compelling recruiting messages:

- How each position helps the department, and by extension the company, achieve its strategic goals

- Which skills are absolutely necessary, and how those skills translate into value for the company

- What elements of each position are attractive, and unattractive, to prospective talent

- Insight into why employees join the company, department, or group, why they stay and why they leave

- Positive and negative attributes of individual managers and their styles

- Any negative perceptions or other hurdles about the group or company that need to be overcome

Here's another reason to align these functions: The talent leader is also a marketer. Whereas your marketing executive is responsible for selling your company's products and services, your talent leader is responsible for selling your company—to Q-Talent. Shouldn't these two leaders spend some time together? It could start as simply as having lunch together a couple of times a month. The more integration between the efforts of the talent and marketing organizations, the better the results will be in terms of crafting the right messages, creatively connecting the dots between the objectives of each group, and presenting a unified, compelling front to all constituencies.

If you believe that your employees are your most strategic asset and you are serious about preserving this asset, start by making your talent leader, or "Chief Talent Officer," part of your executive staff. Make sure that this strategic business leader is responsible for an organization that is focused on hiring and retention, not other general HR functions. With these key resources in place, your talent organization can create the plan that will enable you to effectively address your immediate and long-term needs for Q-Talent.

By combining the insight gained through the talent planning process with the skills, resources, and connections of your best marketing people, your recruiting organization can develop a set of compelling recruitment messages that will help them return new kinds of value to the company. In the next chapter and beyond, we discuss ways to create and deliver those messages to ensure that they not only attract talent, but also help build talent relationships that become more valuable over time.

# 4

# THE CULTURAL OBSESSION OF WORK

---

***Forces in Play:*** *The quest for better jobs becomes a public obsession. Talent is recruited at every opportunity. It takes a finely tuned and targeted talent brand to cut through the clutter.*

*"NOTICE: Men wanted for hazardous journey. Small wages, bitter cold, long months of complete darkness. Constant danger. Safe return doubtful. Honour and recognition in case of success."*

—*Ernest Shackleton*

**N**ot the kind of classified ad you see every day, is it? Although it may send a shudder down the spines of some, it inspired dreams in the minds of others. Only a specific type of person, with a specific set of desires, skills, and abilities, would respond to it. And respond they did.

The ad, which ran in the *London Times* in 1913, was a magnet for its target audience. Shackleton received more than 1,000 responses to it, from which he selected 28 men for his famous journey. In the end, the 1915 *Endurance* expedition became hopelessly stuck in the ice of Antarctica. Lost and presumed dead for months, the men eventually managed to escape the frigid continent. All 28 men made it home safely. Talk about an effective talent force.

In the modern era, there may not be a compelling ideal like "honor" to bring a stream of Q-Talent to your doorstep, but there are other ways to tap into the hopes and desires of your ideal candidates.

## Cutting Through the Clutter—The Importance of a Talent Brand

As the trends described in Chapter 2, "Talent Market Demands," continue to unfold, new opportunities will arise for many, leading to more exciting and, in some cases, difficult career decisions. New types of careers will emerge as the information economy continues to evolve. Changes in demographics will put new pressures on many industries to hire the right talent to meet new opportunities critical to the industries' success—or even to their survival. In developing nations moving to a manufacturing economy, new talent markets will continue to emerge as their working cultures and needs evolve.

In countries affected by the dot-com bust, there will be pent-up demand for job changes as the situation improves, resulting in increased labor market "churn"—a business term coined in the world of magazine subscriptions, where new subscribers must be found at a rate that matches or exceeds the rate at which subscriptions expire to maintain the existing level of revenue. This churn will add complexity to the already-shifting talent market, creating even more openings and signaling that more already-employed individuals are looking for new opportunities.

Another talent market trend, which is building with seismic-like pressure, is the willingness of already-employed individuals—in some cases, happily employed individuals—to consider new opportunities. In the recruiting industry, these individuals are called "passive candidates," an oxymoron describing those who are currently working, who do not have a resumé, and are not actively job searching, but for whom the right opportunity is still attractive.

And there is a subset of "passive candidates" who are inching toward active candidate status. These are the ones reading the Sunday classifieds, surfing Monster.com on their lunch breaks, and casually networking with their friends. These so-called "passive" candidates are only one phone call, informational interview, or invitation to interview away from becoming active candidates.

The constant quest for Q-Talent is seeping into our lives. Job sites, such as Monster.com, HotJobs, Seek.com, and StepStone.com, have succeeded in the challenging dot-com world. Escapeartist.com, Asia-net.com, JM Enterprises (jmep.com), and others provide a clearinghouse for international opportunities. Ads for Monster.com and HotJobs have aired during the Super Bowl, the highest-rated and most expensive advertising forum in the world. Job links are often highlighted on the front page of newspaper Web sites. If you do not think that the talent market is big business, think again.

Even Hollywood has caught on. How many television shows worldwide depict doctors, police, firefighters, teachers, lifeguards, soldiers, private eyes, office workers, and the challenges (not to mention shenanigans) they face at work every day? Award-winning sitcoms, such as the BBC's *The Office*, and reality series, such as A&E's *Airline* and NBC's *The Apprentice*, continue the tradition.

All of these factors—changing demographics, economic upturn, people's appetite for opportunity, broad-reach media—create demand for better opportunities. And this demand is not only driven by MBAs, actors, athletes, engineers, and salespeople anymore. Media and technology bring the concept of ambition—of seeking new opportunities, new careers, and new jobs—to the popular culture.

The result? Attention to work and career opportunities is becoming a new cultural obsession. People are rapidly gaining confidence and spending more time and energy on the lookout, even if it is only casual flirtation. Employees can become bolder in asking for raises or promotions because they know their worth and value. Many will also develop the confidence and ability to market themselves efficiently, resulting in continued job mobility as workers leave their current positions for greener pastures.

Chapter 7, "Talent Goes on Offense," discusses this phenomenon of talent empowerment more completely, but for now, this is a fundamental shift in the talent landscape: It is not that only the employees have power or only the employers have power. It is that knowledge is power. Strategy is power. From now on, more and more people will look at what is happening around them, think ahead, and do what is right for themselves, their families, and their companies.

Companies, facing a persistent need for Q-Talent at every level, need savvy and careful planning to tap into and harness the power and passion behind this new obsession. Unprepared companies will lose their best people to those with a plan for acquiring Q-Talent. Do not count on old-fashioned loyalty to see you through. Too many workers in generations X and Y have seen their parents make huge sacrifices for their careers, spending years, even decades, at a company, only to be laid off. If a cultural institution, such as Japan's concept of "lifetime employment," can die off, then there are no guarantees anywhere anymore.

Just as employees are expected to show up on time every day and produce day in and day out—to continually prove themselves—so will companies find they must continually work to attract and keep their best people. If you take away nothing else from this book, take this hiring and retention imperative seriously and start to plan your talent needs now. The window is closing fast for those who want to be forerunners.

One of the most immediate results of the phenomenon we have been describing is that the marketplace for talent is "noisy"—cluttered with an abundance of employment messages. Some highly desirable candidates might even feel bombarded, chased, or spammed. And with all of the great capabilities afforded by new technology, there will be new generations of technological annoyances, à la the Web browser "pop-up window," for job searchers to overcome. As a result, companies need to find a way to cut through the clutter and do so in a way that helps build a mutually respectful relationship with candidates.

## What Is a Talent Brand?

The challenge to attract attention by differentiating yourself is not a new one, of course.

When it comes to their product or service brands, organizations, especially large companies, generally "get it." In hotly competitive industries, such as retail, companies spend millions establishing their name and creating a strong brand image that compels consumers to reach for their products. A strong brand sets expectations and engenders loyalty. It can overcome price differences, distribution problems, economic turmoil, and public relations debacles. A strong brand influences people. It creates an emotional bond.

Companies with strong brands know who their customers are and how the brand appeals to each group of constituents. They have strategies and messages built around the brand from top to bottom. Strict guidelines determine how the brand is portrayed, reproduced, placed, and talked about. And they make sure the brand is conveyed in all of the organization's communications.

Or do they? Many times, because of the arrogance of supply discussed earlier, companies have not put the same effort into making sure the overall brand is carried through in their efforts to communicate with Q-Talent. They have not defined what makes their organization a unique place to work. They have not mapped out the type of person they want to attract and go after. They have not built messages and programs to go out and get those people. In short, they have not identified or put any work into their "talent brand."

If the reputation of a company's products or services is its face, the talent brand is its heart and soul. It represents the collective goodwill of the people who make the company go. The talent brand is about service, positive interaction, and mutual respect, but it is also about livelihoods, hopes, and aspirations. These qualities are the essence of the talent brand.

Just like a product brand, a company's talent brand builds over time. It can engender the same feelings of desire, the same dreams that a compelling product message brings to life. It can bring tremendous loyalty and, through word of mouth, more traffic to your doorstep.

Over time, the talent brand has persuasive power that the company might not even realize. That is because the biggest single influence on perception has always been word of mouth. If someone has a great experience—or a terrible experience—working for a company, then all of his or her friends will know about it. Then, when the same company comes up in other conversations, those friends will share the experiences they have heard secondhand. Average companies might not feel the results of this phenomenon as much, but companies with great talent-management practices or terrible ones can be sure they are being talked about.

## Getting Started

As with a product brand, creating the right talent brand requires creativity and hard work.

First, recruiting needs to be a strategic imperative for the company, alongside marketing. Whoever is charged with creating your talent brand should collaborate with your marketing team to determine the compelling link between the company, its philosophies, goals, principles, and its talent. What is the essence of the company, and what is it about that essence that makes candidates feel like they want to be a part of it all?

Second, who is your ideal candidate? Find out in as much detail as possible who your target employee is—what she likes to do, what she likes to think about. What special skills and knowledge does she possess? What are her aspirations, her dreams? Take your time with this. Do your homework. Remember, there is growing popular interest in career opportunities. Do you want to spend all your time sifting through unqualified talent? It will be exponentially faster and easier to find your ideal candidates if you know, in detail, exactly who they are.

Third, create a message that speaks to your ideal candidate and, as much as possible, only her. Those of you with marketing expertise may recognize the outlines of a positioning framework in the steps we are describing. If your organization has a positioning framework for its products or services, modify it to serve your talent acquisition purposes. Refer to the list of questions provided in the previous chapter, where we discussed the importance of aligning with marketing to create compelling talent messages.

Some companies have created and communicated an effective talent brand for years. U.S. outdoor equipment outfitter REI has long enjoyed a reputation of providing an engaging work environment and comprehensive benefits. Beyond that, REI also projects an image that automatically attracts the kind of employees the company wants. REI has tapped into the essential appeal of the outdoors and brought that appeal to its talent force as well as its customers. The company's employees buy into REI and its mission because the brand represents them and, in the words of brand guru Scott Bedbury, "provides an emotional context for their lives."

This example reveals another benefit of a talent brand—it is also a screening tool, because applicants will invariably gravitate to talent brands that align with their identities.

Clothing retailer Abercrombie & Fitch is a striking example of this type of candidate/brand alignment. It is tough to imagine many senior citizens applying for work at Abercrombie & Fitch. The company's brand is focused, targeted, and applied with consistency to its recruiting efforts. Look at the company's Web site. Continually updated, it will invariably show you a beautiful, young person on the front page. Enter the site and you'll see another smiling, fit, handsome young face. Enter the job opportunities section and there it is again. By now, the site has shown you three times what you should look like if you want to work at Abercrombie & Fitch.

When used in this way, talent branding images can simultaneously attract your target candidates while dissuading those who might not be as good a fit. For Abercrombie's recruiting, not to mention sales, this finely honed messaging is an undeniable asset. It causes their target employees to want to be a part of it all. They just get it. As a result, walk into any Abercrombie & Fitch store, and you can see the talent brand at work.

Alongside your talent brand imagery, words have the same power to attract the right kind of talent. We started this chapter with a powerful example, the job description that Ernest Shackleton wrote seeking men to join his *Endurance* expedition to Antarctica. A recent example is the message greeting visitors at Nike's career site as of Spring 2004 (italic added for emphasis):

> Nike does more than outfit *the world's athletes*. We are a place to *explore potential, obliterate boundaries*, and *push the edges* of what can be. We are not looking for workers. We're looking for people who can *contribute, grow, think, dream and create*. We *thrive* in a culture that *embraces diversity* and *rewards imagination*. We seek out *achievers, leaders, visionaries*. We love *winners*. At Nike, it is about bringing what you have to *a challenging and constantly evolving game*.

Talk about a "swoosh" statement. Copy like this gives people something to dream about—an ideal brand experience. It shows prospective candidates why Nike needs them, how they fit in, and the opportunities they will have to better themselves if they work there. More importantly, it reflects something that is fundamentally "Nike."

If you are Avis, maybe you write about what it means to "try harder." If you are State Farm Insurance, you might examine how someone can embody the value of truly being there—"like a good neighbor." There is no right or wrong, only what works best to attract the right talent to your company. And to be right for your company, the employment messages should dovetail with the image and brand statements that your marketing team is already putting out there.

# Making It Real

Just like "who a person is" cannot be separated entirely from "what she does," a successful brand goes beyond marketing hyperbole to the reality behind the message.

Your talent brand must reflect your company's reality. When differences occur, it can cause a major disconnect, and there is a risk that new employees will be disillusioned. When companies do not meet the expectations they set forth, their talent brand is doomed. Their clever slogans will ring hollow. Instead of inspiring loyalty, they will inspire feelings of irony, or worse.

If you are starting from scratch to develop a talent brand, then once you commit to truth, the talent brand can fall out of an examination of the company itself, compared with its needs and goals. Examine the product messages, the brand images. Take stock of the company's objectives, as well as those of each department. Look at the business itself and what it takes to build, deliver, and maintain the quality of your products and services. What is special about your company? Examine who your customers are—are they different from or similar to your talent? Chances are, they are similar. If you are recruiting for a specific position or if there is a specific skill set essential to the company, describe the business problem solved by those skills or that position. What is the value to the company of the person you want to hire?

Take the business goals and objectives, the realities that the company faces, and weave them into a story that appeals to exactly the sort of person the company needs. To be effective, the message should create an emotional reaction. It should cause a light to come on inside your ideal talent. Do this, and you will cause your prospective talent to start picturing how their lives might be different if they were working for you.

This process, based on the business realities of the company, will lead to a talent brand and, ultimately, a recruiting strategy aligned with the business model. As a result, the company will begin focusing its efforts on more strategic sourcing and on laying the groundwork for compelling employment messages that derive directly from what the business is trying to accomplish. Think about it. What is more inspiring than a company that knows exactly what you do and how valuable that is to the bottom line?

highly proactive person right away, it is important for the candidate evaluation process to reflect the timeliness and sense of urgency you expect from whoever gets hired.

- Can you compare the profiles of successful people in your company and find the characteristics you are looking for in your candidates? If you profiled such an employee, could you put the information directly inside the job description and have it all make sense?

## Targeting the Effort

As with marketing, after you have determined whom your target audiences are and carefully honed the company's messages to appeal to them, you can start thinking about implementation. The next step is to identify the most effective forum for your recruiting efforts. Where will your messages be delivered? Who is going to read them? Are these the people you are trying to reach?

Go back to the kind of personality and skills you want. You know your customers. Do you know your employees? Which segments of the population fit this mold in high numbers? Where do you find those people?

Many companies do not have an answer to these questions and attempt to cover their bases by carpet-bombing the population with ads in the Sunday paper, national magazines, on large public job boards, on radio or television, and at career fairs. All of these traditional methods, although popular, lack focus. They lack strategy. They are not targeted. As such, they generally provide results, but those results are often cumbersome and unproductive.

These scattershot approaches might or might not find their way to your ideal candidate, but they will almost always find their way to the active (perhaps desperate) candidates who are sending resumés out left and right. These untargeted approaches create more "noise," both for your HR department and for the candidates.

To find your ideal talent, the next difference maker—who is probably a passive candidate, already employed and rarely reading the classifieds or job boards—companies have to be more thoughtful and creative about how they place their employment messages. The goal is to be within arm's reach or, better yet, a keystroke away from your targeted talent.

The companies that win in this game will often be those that find new and refreshing ways to effectively target the talent they seek.

For example, videogames developer and publisher Electronic Arts (EA) included a URL for their careers Web site in each of its game manuals, putting employment messages in the hands of millions of passionate gamers. Think some of them might be qualified and interested in working at EA?

As another example, U.S. defense contractors, such as Harris Corp. and Raytheon, are often challenged to find workers with federal security clearance, which is not a high percentage of the population. Because of this, these companies have taken extensive measures online and offline to get ahead of the game and source this specific type of Q-Talent. In response to the same issue, some recruiting agencies now work for these firms, positioning themselves in close proximity to military outplacement posts, where military personnel are cycling out of their tours of duty. Not arm's reach, but not that far away.

Creative possibilities for targeting talent abound. Think about the people—your customers—who already interact with you and have an interest in the products or services you provide. For example, a movie store could mine its customer database to find the biggest movie buffs—who has rented the most movies over the past few years? Maybe one of them would be interested in a part-time gig that came with some free rentals. The manager could talk to prospective talent about this the next time they visit the store. Short of that direct contact, employment messages could simply be placed on the movie boxes themselves.

Pizza parlors advertise for drivers on their boxes, offering a signing bonus for those with clean driving records. Companies could put employment messages on credit card receipts and potentially catch people twice, once when they sign and again when they reconcile their checkbooks.

Or maybe a country or region is trying to find available talent. New Zealand, with its dire need for medical personnel, could extend the basic advertising it might do in medical journals and at medical conferences by running ads during fishing shows offering free fly-fishing trips to one of the greatest fly-fishing venues in the world, Lake Taupo.

After you have exhausted some immediate opportunities to attract Q-Talent, begin to broaden your reach by launching initiatives that will help your organization cultivate Q-Talent in the long term. Just as some of the most successful marketing initiatives involve long-term partnerships, some industries might benefit from forming symbiotic, cooperative relationships to achieve talent acquisition results years down the line. For instance, a university with a major veterinary program is always competing for top talent—those superstar high school students who want to become veterinarians. At the same time, a company such as Purina also needs to ensure they have talent in the future—the veterinary scientists who create their pet food formulas.

Suppose a major university proposes to Ralston Purina that they jointly run a summer camp for kids interested in becoming vets. The kids get an exciting opportunity to explore a field of interest and perhaps, in a few years, even earn a scholarship. The school gets to identify and build relationships with potential talent. Purina gets a terrific advertising opportunity and a way to identify future talent, knowing that some of those veterinary students will end up on the scientific side.

Taking it a step further, the university and Ralston Purina could then propose to the television network Animal Planet that they run a special on the vet camp program. When the network runs the show, it could display an icon in the corner of the TV screen that directs kids to a Web site where they can learn about the camp, play animal games, and interact with the university or each other. Animal Planet gets a new show for its younger viewers and a new stream of visitors to its Web site. The camp's participation rate explodes. The kids have a blast, and every time the family shops for dog food, they have to at least look fondly at the Ralston Purina bags. Everyone wins.

The talent market of the future has the potential to drive these kinds of arrangements as companies become more creative, more forward thinking, and more strategic in their recruitment efforts. After all, why should these companies pay for separate efforts when a coordinated effort enables them to spend further and deeper with greater results? The types of programs you can create are only limited by your imagination.

Consider the following proactive, strategic steps that other organizations are taking to meet their long-range talent needs:

- Responding to a general lack of skilled workers, a locally owned shop in Lubbock, Texas, has teamed with education leaders to create a program for training automotive technicians. This not only enhances the technicians' education with real-life experience in the company's auto bays; it will also help the business by building a pipeline of trained auto workers in the Lubbock area to meet the demand.

- Medical systems in New Zealand, facing a dire shortage of doctors, are using their career Web sites to establish long-term relationships with medical talent around the world, "selling" the lifestyle in New Zealand as a way to help attract top talent.

- One hospital system in Indiana has created an outreach program for grade school and junior high students to get them thinking about medical careers, outlining how to pursue a career in medicine, and how the hospital can help. The system also has begun to employ a cutting-edge compensation structure that rewards nurses and other critical talent based on merit and performance, as opposed to the classic emphasis on seniority. These programs are both designed to attract and retain young, skilled, and motivated Q-Talent.

- The videogame industry is supporting and helping to create college degree programs to develop the next generation of skilled Q-Talent. This relatively new industry has seen sales of videogames grow beyond Hollywood's box office receipts, yet there is still no widely recognized four-year program to train game developers. In conjunction with public institutions around the world, this industry is now working to develop an entirely new base of skilled workers worldwide.

- Defense contractors in the United States are having more and more difficulty finding U.S. citizens with appropriate technical backgrounds necessary for research, development, and production work. (U.S. citizens are especially needed for jobs requiring security clearance.) Some companies are even considering mergers or acquisitions solely based on their need for experienced talent.

- One of the largest financial services groups in the world has begun tying CEO performance in part to talent objectives. The CEO of each of the group's companies is now required to report on talent management progress and outline future plans.

- Some companies that are offshoring in other parts of the world are establishing relationships with universities in those countries so that they can recruit undergraduates there—talent that will work in those companies abroad or back at home.

- A hospital in Florida invests in educational buildings for nurses at local college campuses and provides scholarships and education assistance, ensuring a steady stream of talent ahead of demand.

- A former biotechnology executive teaches high school biology in the San Francisco Bay Area. He is working with Genentech and other leading biotech firms to be sure that he is teaching his students the "what's" and "how's" that these companies expect from their talent force 4 to 10 years from now.

- A major U.S. college has developed an internship program through which college undergraduates can work in the defense industry and obtain federal security clearance while in school.

- For Jody Conradt, early planning for future talent needs is already a fact of life. Conradt is head coach of the University of Texas women's basketball team. In that business, the coach and her assistants—all of them talent managers—identify and start developing relationships with target Q-Talent when these prospects are 13 or 14 years old. There are strict rules of engagement regarding when, where, and how much contact can be involved. To stay ahead, assistant coaches are on the Internet instant messaging (IM-ing) prospects and watching blogs and chat sites to see where the talent is going and what is being said.

A shortage of auto bay technicians in Lubbock, Texas, might not seem like a big deal, but when a nation's defense industry is having trouble finding the talent it needs to compete and keep up with demand, the potential ramifications should cause business leaders in every industry to pay attention.

Talent development, seen in some of the preceding examples, is one of the fastest growing initiatives inside companies. How much less does it cost to develop talent in-house or in-region? In addition to the development initiatives listed previously, many companies now have their own internal "university" to teach and develop proprietary skills.

Here's one more example: Ross Perot, famed for starting the technology firm Electronic Data Systems (EDS) in the late 1970s, created a Q-Talent force and high-performance culture by offering a three-year training course for his sales staff. He attracted fresh, hardworking individuals who were driven to succeed. Any salesperson who joined was required to sign a three-year contract. Those who left during the three-year period paid back a prorated portion of the training. In this way, Perot put a value on training and talent development. EDS implemented a proactive plan to ensure the right talent would be available externally and internally to match the planned growth of the company. EDS grew successfully due to their careful planning and long-term investment in having the right talent in the right place at the right time.

So, what could you do to draw talent to your company or industry that you are not doing now?

## Using Technology to Reach Talent

Today's technology gives companies a global reach and allows them to easily communicate with people in their living rooms, at their desks, on the subway—almost anywhere someone is willing to be contacted. Companies have explored and exploited these technologies to help create value in their sales forces, technology services, supply chains, customer service, and repair departments.

In the arena of talent, however, many of the efficiencies to be gained from modern communication have remained untapped. The technology exists, but companies have not been thinking about ways to take advantage of it when it comes to finding and acquiring talent. As the heat gradually turns up on recruiters, as arrogance of supply becomes a relic of the past, and as companies start realizing the huge bottom-line potential of great talent management, more creativity and energy will be put into finding new ways to recruit the best people. Technology can, and will, play an ever-growing role in that effort.

Let's take a look at how a company might use technology to reach and recruit talent today. A candidate might see an employment ad during the Super Bowl at halftime, for example. First, he gets the not-so-subtle message that what he is doing for his livelihood is sub-par to what he could be doing—the famous Monster.com campaign featured children saying such things as, "When I grow up, I want to sit in the same cubicle for 20 years." Next, he sees an ad for a financial services firm that contains the URL for that company's career site.

His curiosity piqued, the candidate gets on the Internet while he's watching his team get blown out in the third quarter. It just so happens that the financial services firm has a position of interest. He answers a few easy questions, submits the questionnaire electronically, and by the end of the game, he has an e-mail telling him he is qualified and the company is interested.

At dinner the next night, he is talking with his partner about the wonderful opportunity he might have at this other company. By Friday, when his boss thinks he wants to talk about last week's Super Bowl game over a drink, he instead tells the story of his fantastic new opportunity, and asks how badly the company wants him to stay.

Communication channels are not limited to television, e-mail, and the Web. In the first half of 2005, there were more than 170 million cell phone users in the United States, and far more in Europe and Asia. Instead of passing notes in class, teenagers text message one another. Some handheld games can access online gaming communities from anywhere.

Nokia's N-Gage device, a hybrid gaming console-telephone-PDA, enables players to share profiles and participate in chats and message boards. Some people feel lost without their "crackberry." Google is a verb. Sixty seconds is too long to wait on hold.

In this nearly always-on, always-ready environment, it will not be long before savvy recruiters make increasingly effective use of the myriad communications channels to reach Q-Talent candidates at all levels with compelling job opportunities.

A talent brand strategically aligned with your business is a huge competitive advantage. Similar to the way a marketer runs a marketing campaign, recruiters need to understand the habits, hopes, and dreams of their engineers, longshoremen, and fry cooks, and develop a talent brand that reaches out to them to make an effective "sale."

Coupled with targeted online and offline delivery, a talent brand has the potential to cut through the "noise" and reach your desired Q-Talent. To effectively communicate their talent brand, companies should make an ongoing investment in exploring and using technology. The next chapter shows how companies can harness technology to create talent communities where they can promote their talent brands, meet their ongoing talent needs, and contribute new forms of business value to the organization.

# 5

# BUILDING A TALENT COMMUNITY

---

*Forces in Play: Everyone is available all the time, waiting for the next opportunity to come along and capture his or her attention. The Web is the recruiting weapon of choice.*

---

After the September 11, 2001, terrorist attacks in the United States, the travel industry went through a period of plummeting performance. Airlines, cruise ships, and other recreation industries began laying off hordes of workers to stem their hemorrhaging cash flows. During this period, Royal Caribbean Cruise Lines took an unusual and strategic approach—the company intensified its efforts to build relationships with candidates over the Internet. Why did Royal Caribbean begin recruiting while simultaneously laying off people?

The answer is simple logic. Knowing that companies across the industry, including Royal Caribbean itself, were laying people off, Royal Caribbean officials decided to send these newly unemployed professionals a simple message: We cannot hire you today, but we want to know you, because there will be a time when we will be hiring again.

Royal Caribbean transformed the rapid downturn into a competitive opportunity. The company put the processes in place so that when the industry began to recover, they would already have a handle on whom they wanted to hire, be in open communication with those people, and therefore be able to deploy a new talent force faster and more effectively than their competitors, putting them in a stronger position to quickly exploit the upturn.

Royal Caribbean understood that Q-Talent is always hard to get. Rather than sit back and then react when the economy improved, Royal Caribbean was proactive. Their talent organization used the company's Web site to increase its reach. They developed a private, virtual "talent community," which soon included tens of thousands of people all over the world. They encouraged former employees as well as others in the industry to join the online community so that the company could keep in touch with them. The ensuing communications were honest, forthright, and mutually beneficial.

When the time came, the company was well ahead of their talent demand—and the competition. When the cruise industry began to recover, Royal Caribbean had direct relationships with a huge pool of qualified and available talent. The company was able to hire at a faster rate and gear up to capacity much more quickly than it would have without its strategic efforts, giving it a tremendous competitive advantage. Even more impressive, the company accomplished this while decreasing its utilization of talent agencies *by 90 percent*, saving millions of dollars in the process.

This is just one example where a strategic talent organization, aligned with business objectives, used technology and great messaging to bring tremendous value to the company—not only in terms of the size of its available pool of talent and the rate at which it could bring quality people aboard when necessary, but also in terms of what it contributed directly to the bottom line.

## Forming Technology-Enabled Relationships

By now, you have developed a talent organization that is closely aligned with the business and poised to deliver business value. You have reached out and partnered with your company's best marketing minds to create a talent brand and accompanying talent-specific messages. You are starting to see a return on those efforts as your messages bring new talent "window shopping" through your employment-related Web pages.

What do you know about these "window shoppers?" These are people who have become interested in your company and stopped by to take a virtual look. Perhaps they are responding directly to one of your messages. Regardless of how they found you, there is value, intrigue, and opportunity in the mere fact that these people have come to your Web site and looked for job openings and other information about your company.

Each visitor responded in some way to your company's employment brand image. Many of these visitors likely share work interests and employment philosophies. They all have the most important thing in common—they want to work for you. This is a community of common interest. It is a community of potential talent and also of potential shareholders, customers, and evangelists. It is a community of potential value in more ways than one. As you will see in this chapter, a talent community is a new resource that your organization can utilize in flexible and creative ways to solve myriad business challenges.

So, what are you going to do with it?

You are going to acknowledge it, build it, and nurture it. You are going to fold it into your talent plan, formulate goals around it, and measure it. Like all relationships, interacting with your talent community is not a one-time event or a one-way street, but rather an ongoing process involving give-and-take. As with any professional relationship, to foster mutual respect and sow the seeds of a long-term, mutually beneficial partnership, you need to be smart, strategic, and—most of all—*gracious* in how you approach your talent community.

Clearly, this is a new type of relationship that goes beyond the realm of traditional HR, where you are working to manage your employees. Now you have got to think about relating to the individuals in your talent community as current talent, alumni, customers, business partners, and of course, that all-important prospective Q-Talent.

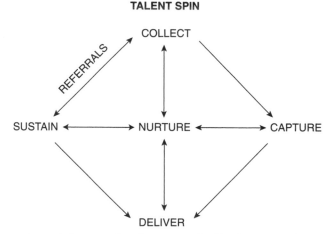

The talent spin cycle is a continual process of collecting new talent prospects, forming relationships with them, and either qualifying them for delivery into the organization or maintaining the relationships over time so that you can consider them for future opportunities.

# The "Sticky" Talent Web: Collecting Participants

For companies that want to stay ahead, engaging with their talent community is a never-ending process. The "talent spin" is a cycle of continually updating your Web site and "pushing" your messages online and offline to attract, or "pull," new talent to your site. In the Collect phase of this cycle, your Web site is truly like the spider's web. Although you will not be devouring your talent for breakfast, you do want to make the experience on your site "sticky" enough that more visitors will be compelled to stay for awhile.

What happens when potential talent submits a resume on your careers site? Giving you the benefit of the doubt, we will assume your system automatically e-mails the person an acknowledgment. This e-mail is the first direct communication your company has with that talent. Does it say, "Welcome to our talent community"? Or does it say, "We will call you if something comes up"? Does it reaffirm the company's brand? If you are not sending a reply at all, what does that say about your organization and what it might be like to work there?

If your employment Web site leads to a one-way resumé-submittal page or visitor profile page, it might not matter what you say. Typically, these types of pages ask for personal information, ostensibly to be stored and accessed later. Only active job seekers will take the time to fill out these forms. These people are usually either unemployed or unhappy in their current situation. They might be great talent, but active job seekers represent, at most, 20 percent of your available talent pool. And even within that 20 percent, most are only looking out of curiosity. They simply want information they can use, think about, and dream about before making a major life change.

As a result, companies with straightforward resumé-submittal pages find that as many as 98 percent of visitors to that page "back out" without submitting anything. Most never return. Their reasons vary. Maybe they have had a good job for five years and do not have a current resumé. Maybe they just wanted to learn about jobs at your company to find out whether it is a good fit before actually applying for one. Maybe they just do not want to give you their phone number over the Internet.

Are these the kinds of people you want to be turning away?

The bottom line is, a 2 percent return means that you are losing the opportunity to engage 98 out of every 100 people who visit your Web site. What if you were a retailer or a restaurant and 98 percent of the people who came through your door never bought anything? Companies should expect a much higher rate of success from their Web recruitment efforts. How does a 20 percent rate of return sound? 30 percent? If 1,000 people visit the site, that is the difference between 200 and 300. Think you might have a better chance of finding that next superstar if you can choose from 100 more people with the same amount of effort? For large companies, those numbers could be much higher.

In the virtual world, your lobby can hold thousands of people without violating any fire codes. Web technology enables companies to communicate and build relationships with thousands of people located all over the world. So instead of throwing up roadblocks, such as, "Give me a current resumé," why not simply invite them in? Attracting and communicating with talent online does not necessarily take a big investment as much as a change in philosophy. Being gracious, respectful, and, most of all, responsive to the people who visit your site will go a long way. Being targeted, strategic, and honest with your messages will take you even further.

Today's interactive technology can provide an experience that is much more like traditional recruitment—ask prospects about their interests, match positions to those interests, e-mail prospects data that is interesting enough to get them to take the next step in the process. Online, this interaction can lead to a valuable relationship without requiring candidates to give you their name, address, or other personal information.

To maximize this collection phase, ask for as little as possible. Make the "cost of entry" as low as you can. It is all about the candidate at this point. Offer them some value (for example, information, a discount, an upgrade, or a coupon). Give them the option to remain anonymous. Let them know your philosophy regarding their potential relationship with your organization, the choices they have for engaging with you, and how you honor and protect them by letting them choose to give you information when they want. Some of this information will be contained in the privacy policy you should link to from each page on your site, but you should also articulate the value of the relationship more prominently in concise, simple language. If you offer them something, follow through immediately, at least with an e-mail confirmation.

The site should explain the value that the organization places on great talent and how, because of that priority, you want to know them. You want to know what they do, and what they are dreaming about doing. And you want to stay in touch. You do not need their phone number, you do not need to know where they live. All you need is an e-mail address. If you can obtain someone's anonymous, non-work–related e-mail address and then use it to communicate respectfully and graciously with the person, you are on your way to establishing a successful, long-term relationship with that person.

This kind of open approach, requiring a low investment by the candidate, is the key to attracting any potential candidate, including a passive one. Remember, the passive candidate is an oxymoron used to describe the person who is not technically "looking," but who might become interested in an opportunity if his or her attention is piqued. These prospective candidates are typically wary and desire a high degree of anonymity, which in turn requires trust. Therefore, to be successful, your Web site's content and interactions need to provide a way for persons to engage with you on their terms, slowly, in a way that makes them comfortable and willing to return to your site again.

## Stuck in the Web: Capturing the Relationship

Asked for as little as their first name, e-mail address, and areas of interest, visitors to your employment pages are more likely to spend the required 60 seconds—or less—to give you this information. After that short, quick, easy registration has been submitted, you have just captured a talent relationship. If your Web site copy and processes are working correctly, you will soon find yourself with an ever-growing community of talent that you can begin to nurture for the long term.

With this resource, you do not necessarily have to run a newspaper ad every time your organization has a new job opening. You do not have to comb through dozens, even hundreds, of resumés when you need to fill a position. You do not have to reinvent the wheel every time you want to hire someone. You can now begin to meet your talent needs by reaching out to your talent community, potential candidates who have shown a sincere interest in your company.

Over time, you can begin to find out more about each participant. For example, your communications can become more targeted with candidates who select high-demand skill areas during registration or in subsequent communications, or who demonstrate other interesting skills during their participation in your talent community.

In the meantime, stay in touch with these folks regularly, but not too frequently. You want your talent looking forward to your communications. Some companies use a two-month cycle, communicating general information to the entire talent community three times per year and sending job opportunities and other more targeted content to high-value candidates an additional three times per year. Or, as part of registration, allow people to indicate how often they would like to hear from you.

Your communications should continue to provide something of value, be it an entertaining read, useful information, special offers, or something else. You have to provide value first to gain value down the line. You might send messages from the CEO, company news, or other company-specific updates such as upcoming product launches, special events, or sales.

Every communication to your talent community should contain a value statement about talent. You do not necessarily need to come right out and say, "We value talent," but rather highlight the company's benefits, commitment to workers, and any best-place-to-work awards or other evidence of that commitment.

As job opportunities open up, e-mail them to specific participants in your talent community who might be interested and include links back to the company's site. When candidates click the link that you provide in your e-mail, it should automatically take them to a Web page that asks specific questions about their qualifications while providing more information about the job in question. The next section describes these questions in more detail.

This stage is where Web recruitment offers real value and efficiency. With current Web technology, the technologist in your talent organization, described in Chapter 3, "Building a Competitive Talent Organization," can design a front-end solution that automatically screens candidates. "Front-end solution" might sound fancy and expensive, but like most business-efficiency initiatives, it is actually a huge money-saver in terms of both actual expenditures and productivity.

For some companies, initial candidate screening is a significant expense. Think back to the product manager working 70 hours per week. Instead of asking him to screen candidates by wading through a stack of resumés, the Web site can do most of that for him. The site will deliver prescreened, prequalified talent to the product manager's desktop, along with some personal information about the candidate that he can use to start the conversation.

Your talent organization can also be a bit leaner now. If you currently utilize agency recruiting, this is a classic technology benefit story. You can transfer just about all of the initial screening activities performed by the agency to the Web site and allow the expensive contract recruiters to focus solely on delivering qualified candidates to your organization, providing an immediate return on your investment in the Web site.

Without using the Web to prescreen candidates, a large company might need to retain 50 or more external recruiters, even with state-of-the-art technology tools, just to handle the effort of qualifying and delivering talent into the organization. With contract recruiters often commanding $7,000 to $12,000 or more per month, that is an expense of $4 to $7.2 million per year, largely to perform the functions you have just automated. Using the approach previously described, most businesses will see these costs decrease significantly, even dramatically. How about reducing your outsourced recruiting headcount from 50 to 10?

What's more, those 10 recruiters, whether internal or external, will be able to bring a higher level of value to the business. It starts with the efforts described in Chapter 3. Freed from the task of initial screening, the talent organization can now work on extending its reach, both within the walls of the business and beyond them, developing and strengthening the talent strategy, brand, messages, and philosophy.

The talent organization can spend more time engaging with talent, building affinities, deepening relationships, and bringing talent from cyberspace to the workplace and possibly into one of your open positions.

This type of screening automation also has the potential to improve candidate relations. Imagine this scenario: A high-level technical job opening is automatically published to your company's Web site at 11:50 p.m. A great candidate happens to be online, working late, and receives an automated e-mail about it. He thinks, what the heck, clicks the link in the e-mail, answers the questions on your Web site, and submits the requested information at 12:15 a.m. He passes the initial automated screening process and, as the next step in the process, the system automatically forwards his information to the hiring manager, who is still online after submitting the job less than half an hour ago.

That hiring manager could pick up the phone, knowing the candidate is awake, and contact him to begin a conversation based on information the candidate just provided. Or the hiring manager could immediately send the candidate a short e-mail, expressing his interest in the candidate and scheduling time to talk. Do you think that potential Q-Talent would be impressed with the hiring manager's responsiveness? How long would that process have taken, and what would it have cost, using traditional recruiting means?

## Qualifying the Candidate

Let's take a closer look at the initial screening process we have been discussing. When the candidate reaches a point where she wants to apply online for a position of interest, the company can determine whether there is a match by asking qualifying questions (QQs) online that are specific to each position. At this point in the process, if the person is serious about applying for a position, she will be willing to spend a few minutes answering some questions about her work life. Think of these questions as your "sieve"—if they do their job, all the water and sediment will fall through, and you'll be left with a few shiny gold nuggets.

The tone and format of the QQs should be carefully planned to match the attitude and culture you want to convey, while at the same time obtaining the information you need. If done right, this optional, short form will not be a stressful burden or hassle for your talent, but an interesting, maybe even fun experience that reaffirms their excitement about the opportunity to become a part of your company.

Draw in candidates with compelling, interesting questions that put forth the company's values. To do this, part of each question should contain a statement about the company's commitment to its people or why the position is critical to the company's success. For example, "We are committed to providing the best intensive care facility in the tri-state area. Do you have experience leading a talented, disciplined nursing staff in a highly demanding environment?" If it fits your talent brand, use a quirky bit of wisdom, humor, or whatever style reflects your company's culture: "Our keyboards will shock you if you type less than 60 words per minute. Can you hack it?" The statement can also underline the importance of the skill you are asking about: "We move six tons of product per day. Our people are in great shape. We need people who love exercise and can handle a fast-paced environment."

To craft the questions, the recruiter should work with the hiring manager to hammer out the specifics about the open position. Writing effective questions requires the ability to ask compelling questions combined with an understanding of the mentality and requirements necessary to do the job. Be sure each question will uncover the type of information you need. The entire questionnaire should align with the specific business goals that the position is meant to help accomplish.

---

### The Benefits of Automated Qualifying Questions

The following list, provided by the recruitment firm Novotus, outlines some key areas where good qualifying questions can help the business save time and money in finding the right candidate:

- Automated screening questions conserve the most expensive of all recruiting resources—a recruiter's time. The bottom-line savings are often significant.

- When interacting with your private talent community, any loss of reputation or damage to the talent brand usually

---

results from a lack of communication with the candidate. The QQs, teamed with an automated response system, allow you to get information to the candidate quickly.

- QQs can help flush out any illegitimate applicants by forcing the candidate to either know the information or lie about it. The system quickly uncovers those who embellish.

- QQs facilitate verification of the applicant's location, access to work, and ability to work.

- QQs facilitate candidate ranking based on skills and experience.

- QQs facilitate rapid deployment, and not simply through process automation. For instance, you might have a QQ that states the pay rate, employment status, length of engagement, and other key job attributes. Candidates who agree to these can be routed through the system more quickly.

- QQs aid with recruiting compliance requirements: All candidates are qualified equally, and decisions made at the first level of screening are retained for easy compliance reporting and tracking.

In designing your questions, make sure you have covered all the bases. The following categories describe the information your QQs need to uncover for initial screening purposes:

- **Why do.** "Why do" questions have their roots in the company's mission and values and should evaluate whether the candidate is a good fit for the company's culture. These are often essay-style questions that will help you sort through and talk to candidates after they are qualified.

- **Want to do.** "Want to do" generally uncovers job experience and the applicant's understanding of and enthusiasm for the role. Here, too, essay-style questions may be most useful.

- **Willing to do.** "Willing to do" often involves special qualifiers for such things as odd shifts, occupational hazards, or relocation. It might also get at specific demands of the job, such as the ability to travel, work as a team, or work alone for long stretches.

- **Able to do or Have done**. These questions are typically experience-, training-, skills-, or education-oriented. They also frequently deal with the applicant's availability and location. Often these are "knock-out" questions. If the position requires five years of experience, the system can be set to eliminate candidates with less than five years of experience. If the applicant must reside in Eritrea, the site can be set up to eliminate any non-Eritreans who apply (and automatically send them an e-mail letting them know why they are not being considered).

- **Prove can do**. This is another category of questions that are often necessary to get at specific skills. Maybe this is where you ask for a link to the candidate's doctoral thesis, offer a quiz or a riddle to test their understanding of quantum physics, or ask them to take an online typing exam.

With all of these questions, begin with the business goals that the job function solves, along with the characteristics valued by the department. Keep the underlying message positive and positioned to sell the company's strengths as a recruiter and employer.

If a company decides to use a Web screening system, these questions are the key element in allowing the site to deliver interested, qualified, and available talent to the recruiters' and hiring managers' desktops. With the preceding recommendations and a little practice, the professionals in your talent organization should be able to create an initial screening system with questions that effectively perform this stage of the recruiting process.

When in place, these questions can also help the company adhere to Equal Employment Opportunity Commission and Office of Federal Contract Compliance Programs guidelines. As an automated screening tool, this method creates a "blind" system, where all applicants are treated exactly the same based on their skills, experiences, and goals.

## Sample Qualifying Questions

The following are actual qualifying questions taken from a site that was seeking a retail merchandise planner. The "desired answers" are behind-the-scenes requirements utilized by the software to screen applicants. Based on the "desired answer," some of the candidate's answers are immediately disqualified, whereas others require further evaluation:

I have _____ years experience as a Retail Merchandise Planner.
**Desired Answer:** Minimum of 2.5

I have developed location plans by department based on trend, store profiles, competition, and seasonal conversion issues.
**Desired Answer:** True

I have identified location growth opportunities and minimized down-trending businesses.
**Desired Answer:** True

I am experienced with the analytical skills that are necessary for this position.
**Desired Answer:** True

I can effectively plan and control inventories at the location level to maximize sales, inventory, and profit within management guidelines.
**Desired Answer:** True

I have worked for the following company(s) as a Retail Merchandise Planner: _____.
**Desired Answer:** Requires individual evaluation

I have planned and erected commercial displays, such as those in windows and interiors of retail stores and at trade exhibitions.
**Desired Answer:** True

In my own words this is what a Retail Merchandise Planner is challenged with doing on a day-to-day basis: _____.
**Desired Answer:** Requires individual evaluation

If I were hiring for this position the key attributes that are required are: _____.

**Desired Answer:** Requires individual evaluation

I am qualified for this position for this reason(s): _____.

**Desired Answer:** Requires individual evaluation

These qualifying questions are focused on the categories "Able to do," "Have done," and "Prove can do." Think how much more informative these could be with a few more probing questions to understand "Why do," "Want to do," and "Willing to do."

# New Alliances, New Opportunities, New Ways to Add Business Value

In addition to providing you with great new professionals for your organization, your talent community is an audience available to participate in creative new programs. If you understand your talent community members, their interests, activities, hopes, and dreams, you can create endless programs, initiatives, events, promotions, and strategic partnerships that provide true value to your talent community—and new returns to your business that most companies have never even considered.

For instance, in sports entertainment network ESPN's reality television show, *Dream Job*, contestants took a crash course in sports journalism, vying for a one-year contract with the network. How many people began to think about a career in sports journalism as a result of that show? How many visited ESPN.com to fantasize about their own dream job? Here is a community united behind a common interest—they all dream of becoming an ESPN sportscaster. As with any good talent brand, the TV show, Web site, and accompanying messages probably lead people to self-select for this dream job, distilling this audience to a reasonably focused demographic.

What other common interests might this demographic share? Imagine if ESPN took this programming a step further and began building an online community. Might other companies be interested in the potential of that community? Perhaps companies such as Calloway Golf or Nike would be interested in pursuing a sponsorship or exchanging links with this site, knowing there is a steady flow of people there who fit their target market. Could campaigns, events, or promotions be built around those participants?

These cooperative principles can work in almost any industry. A videogame development company could build a large talent community of people who enjoy playing videogames. Through special promotions, discounts, and other offers, the company could continue to deepen the relationship with each participant, return something of value to the talent community, and at the same time accomplish some of its own recruiting goals.

Perhaps the company needs to move units of a particular game to meet sales expectations or make room for new inventory. They could spur sales by offering a discount to their talent community, returning something of value to the community in the process. Perhaps they need feedback on a beta release of a new game in development. They could invite the talent community to participate in the beta, make all of the participants feel like insiders, and gain useful product data to aid with development. Along the way, they could identify participants who provide exceptional beta feedback, perhaps asking those individuals to come back and preview more new games.

In this scenario, the head of the talent organization would work in tandem with the heads of marketing, sales, product development, and other leaders to affect the number of units sold, revenue streams, product quality, and the company's stock price. Now your talent organization is no longer overhead but is returning real, measurable value to your bottom line.

Technology is a tool. Used strategically, this tool enables you to create and nurture a talent community that will provide an ongoing source of Q-Talent, strengthen your talent brand, and achieve other business results across the organization. Most people work. Most companies hire. Using the Internet to link the two is a bandwagon that everyone should be jumping on.

# 6

# TANGIBLE TALENT
# MEASUREMENT

*Forces in Play:* Smart companies realize a competitive
advantage by measuring their talent efforts to help them
improve. Shareholders, analysts, and business leaders
factor new talent measurements into investment strategies
and policy decisions. State and local governments explore
talent-oriented economic programs.

**W**hat if we told you that excellence in recruiting and retention could increase your organization's market value by 8 percent?

Here's what that would look like:

| Market Value | Market Value Improvement Opportunity |
| --- | --- |
| $250K | $20K |
| $500K | $44K |
| $1M | $80K |
| $10M | $800K |
| $100M | $8M |
| $500M | $40M |
| $1B | $80M |
| $5B | $400M |
| $15B | $1.2B |

Not a bad improvement for your shareholders, is it? Of course, the vast majority of businesses are worth less than the amounts in this chart. But improving recruiting and retention offers an opportunity to create value in businesses of any size.

To some, the value of Q-Talent is common sense—a company filled with tenured, satisfied, productive, hardworking, and smart people is going to perform better and eventually be worth more than a company filled with bitterness, indolence, and rampant turnover. This is true whether you are a multinational corporation or a barbershop.

Although the notion that business competitiveness is tied closely to talent may seem intuitive, social scientists have spent a great deal of time proving it. The decade from 1993 to 2003 saw many studies from researchers, such as Yeung and Berman, Pfeffer, and Ostroff, that used complex statistics to paint a mathematical picture of the correlation.

The 8 percent figure in the chart at the beginning of this chapter came from one of the more dramatic demonstrations of talent valuation, the Watson Wyatt Human Capital Index Study. This study compared a comprehensive Human Capital Index score—a rating of a company's human capital management practices—against financial performance and market value from 1999 to 2001. More than 750 companies from across the United States, Canada, and Europe participated, each with 1,000 or more employees and more than $100 million in revenue or market value.

According to the study, "a significant improvement" in the category "recruiting and retention excellence" accounted for an 8 percent increase in market value. The study defines its standard for "significant improvement" as *one point on a five-point scale*. Considering that many of the companies in the study were worth between $4 billion and $8 billion, that one-point improvement could presumably be worth $40 to $80 million.

So why don't more businesses rank talent capital as their top priority for success? Why don't business leaders treat their talent with the same sense of urgency they give to raw materials, infrastructure, technology, and other business-critical assets? Why do CEOs say, "Talent is the most important thing in our company," and then not make anyone inside the organization responsible for a strategic competitive model that ensures they have the right talent, in the right place, at the right time?

The answer to these questions is, in part, because most companies do not measure talent. It is paradoxical. Businesses love data. Most are swimming in it. Every viable business has a budget and a balance sheet. Its leaders know how much the organization earns and how much it spends. Many have committed to memory the amount of this year's technology investment, this month's price increase in a key raw material—to the penny—or the offer extended in a recent negotiation. Some carry around "scorecards" with regularly updated business indicators. The numbers help them gauge the health of the organization and can be an early warning system for problems and opportunities.

Why don't more companies measure their hiring and retention effectiveness and report and improve on it? Some organizations do, including professional sports teams and companies in the entertainment industry. For the former, ticket sales, wins and losses, hits and flops, strikeouts and home runs provide all the Q-Talent measurements the industry needs. Reflecting the importance of these metrics, most talent scouts for professional sports are paid huge sums. A book published by Michael Lewis in 2004, *Moneyball: The Art of Winning an Unfair Game*, has generated controversy by proposing a new set of metrics by which to predict a baseball team's chances for success. Teams that adhere to Lewis's metrics are said to be playing "moneyball," whereas others dismiss his approach and sabermetrics in general.

For most businesses, innovation in talent capital management represents one of the last great business opportunities, a chance to get ahead and give your company something that your competitors do not have. As indicated in Chapter 2, "Talent Market Demands," accurately measuring an organization's talent represents a major trend that is already beginning to unfold.

Talent measurement can help businesses operate more nimbly. It can generate immediate and substantial cost savings. It can return value. And most important, over time, it can help you put the best talent force in place for the future of your business.

## Talent Metrics

Talent measurement is an extension of business management. This concept has been around for decades. After World War II, W. Edwards Deming took his manufacturing philosophies to Japan and, by measuring productivity, was able to move a motivated business environment and talent force to the forefront of global economic success.

Talent metrics require that the base components of the business model are measured first. If a company knows what it takes to produce a product, they can then align these business metrics with the appropriate talent metrics. The talent leader must understand this sequence to tie talent metrics to real business needs or purposes:

1. First, establish clear business goal(s).

2. Then, define business measurements: What does it take to reach the goal?

3. Create talent measurements: What is needed from each position to succeed?

Studies, such as the Watson Wyatt Human Capital Index Study described in the previous section, will create more pressure to measure talent capital and human resources effectiveness as a way to provide another key indicator of financial success (or the potential for it). Companies will find that there is increasing value—market value—in being able to articulate how they are going to attract better people, how the people they already have in place are superior, how they are going to retain those people, and what their succession plans are. If a company can show that it has better talent, which in turn means it is in a better position for success, how could an investor ignore that?

But on the other side, how can a company articulate those things? What measurements set one company apart from another when it comes to something as intangible as "talent"?

Let's look more closely at how specific talent metrics can help businesses plan for upcoming challenges and opportunities and prevent talent-driven disasters, such as unhealthy turnover or egregious employee behavior.

## Planning for Future Talent Gaps at All Levels

As you read in Chapter 3, "Building a Competitive Talent Organization," the talent leader needs to be closely aligned with other senior managers in your organization. We suggested holding senior managers accountable for this partnership by measuring their participation and contributions in the talent arena. Here are five ways that senior managers can contribute to your organization's talent goals:

- **Plan vigorously**. Senior managers should partner with the talent leader and hiring managers in their division to create a written plan for how they will meet your current and long-term talent needs. Planning for the talent agenda should be as thorough and as vigorous as any other planning in the company (for instance, strategic, annual operating, material, and financial planning). Chapter 3 covers talent planning at length.

- **Be accessible**. Senior managers should schedule regular meetings with their talent organization counterpart and be available and responsive when the talent leader contacts them. All senior managers should be accessible to meet prospective talent anywhere and anytime.

- **Sell**. With a plan in place, senior managers are responsible for "selling" the plan within their division. How will the talent plan help the division succeed? How should people participate? How will they be measured and rewarded for their participation? Senior managers need to emphasize the importance of Q-Talent and back up their words with concrete plans and metrics. They also need to always wear their "selling shoes" when talking and meeting with prospective talent. If a hiring manager or other employee cannot sell his own company to a candidate, then leave that person off of the interview or meeting schedule.

- **Benchmarking**. Know how effective your talent efforts are today and continue to measure these efforts using the metrics outlined next to gauge your efforts over time. Are they working? Also, continuously benchmark internal and external talent. The grass is hardly as green on the other side as you want to believe. Still, knowing who is out there, what they are doing, and how your internal talent stacks up is an essential element of strategic talent planning.

- **Make movement happen**. Don't let open positions stagnate while hiring managers churn through reams of resumés from unqualified candidates. The framework provided in this book shows you how to be proactive in assessing and meeting your talent needs. Put the time and resources behind this framework to make it happen in your organization. And be willing to open up positions and make churn happen within the organization to accommodate new candidates and grow existing talent. Keeping the place moving will add the extra adrenaline needed for all talent to see a future in front of them in the current organization.

What talent metrics can help you in your efforts to find and acquire Q-Talent? Short term, it starts with every hiring manager and recruiter tracking their talent inventory and process: how many open positions they are responsible for, how many resumés they have reviewed, how many informational and formal interviews they have conducted, how many upcoming interviews are scheduled, and time-to-hire for each position. Senior managers need to follow up and manage this information for the open positions in their divisions to make sure that hiring managers and recruiters are actively working to fill open slots and to get a sense of the quantity and quality of talent available for various types of positions—just like they would for an important product delivery.

If certain positions take an unusually long time to fill, recruiters should be closely partnering with the hiring managers for these positions and discussing why this is happening and what to do about it. You might need a separate talent plan (see Chapter 3) for targeting and attracting candidates with difficult-to-find skill sets. Remember, your goal is to move from "reacting" to open positions to proactively cultivating relationships so that the right talent is available to you when you need it, or just before.

To this end, in addition to short-term metrics about current open positions, you need to measure your long-term progress toward building relationships and establishing a pipeline of Q-Talent for future openings. To get to *10* Q-Talent hires, you need to find *1* new person who is not in your pipeline, recruit *6* people from your existing pipeline quickly, and continue to manage relationships with *3* people who will fill your future pipeline and be great hires for future openings. Beyond the 10 people who you hire, you will decide not to hire countless others who express interest in your organization.

Let's look at these four categories and ways to measure your progress in each:

*1. New Talent That You Must Find (About 10% of Your Pipeline)*

| Question | Metric |
|---|---|
| How many new candidates do you need? | Number of new candidates you need to find by level (for example, entry-level, middle-management, executive), role (for example, marketing manager, engineer, quality assurance, finance), and skill set (for example, programming languages, years of management experience). |

| | |
|---|---|
| Which methods for finding new Q-Talent are most effective? | Response rates for all recruiting tactics: Web site, advertising in all media and direct-mail pieces, job fairs, or other recruiting events, referrals, and so on. |
| How long is it taking you to find the types of talent you need? | Rate of talent acquisition by level, role, and skill set. |
| How can you become a "magnet" for the type of talent you seek? | Make sure that any new recruiting initiatives include relevant metrics, including long-range initiatives to nurture talent relationships at an early stage (for example, talent development partnerships with colleges or high schools). |

*2. Talent That Finds You and That You Want to Hire Immediately (About 60% of Your Pipeline)*

| Question | Metric |
|---|---|
| How does this talent find you? | Response rates for all recruiting tactics: Web site, advertising in all media and direct-mail pieces, recruiting events, referrals, talent community registration, and so on. |
| How quickly do you respond to qualified talent? | Turnaround time for candidate inquiries received via Web site, e-mail, phone, snail mail, referrals, and events. |
| Are you capable of managing qualified candidates from first contact to hire? | Time-to-hire and possibly candidate satisfaction (via surveys given to new hires). |

*3. Talent That Finds You and That You Want to Hire, Not Now but for Future Openings (About 30% of Your Pipeline)*

Ask the same questions as number 2, above, plus the following:

| Question | Metric |
|---|---|
| How long will you cultivate the relationship? | Length of relationship from first contact (while the relationship is underway). Length of relationship from first contact to hire or first contact to disengagement (due to the candidate finding another new job, growing impatient or losing interest). |
| How will you balance the candidates' timing versus your timing? | Readiness to turn on spigot when the timing is right. |

*4. Talent That Comes to You—Who You Do Not Want to Hire*

| Question | Metric |
|---|---|
| How do you decline these candidates while ensuring that they send you referrals? How can you decline them graciously? | Time-to-decision and time-to-follow-through communication. |
| Can you manage/handle their referrals? | Conversion rate. Number of repeat referrals. |

Remember, all candidates, even people you do not hire, have value to your organization as referrers of talent, customers of your products and services, market influencers, and stockholders. Therefore, through your talent practices, you should treat each candidate with respect and care. Chapter 8, "Relationship Recruiting (Still) Rules," talks more about the importance of gracious recruiting.

After talent is on board, additional metrics can help your organization track its talent management practices, including succession planning and identifying potential talent-related issues, such as turnover and serious employee misbehavior.

## Succession Planning

Planning for future talent gaps at the executive level requires special consideration because these positions are both highly strategic and high-profile. We provided an example of solid succession planning at the beginning of Chapter 1, "The Quality Talent Imperative," by describing how GE prepared for former CEO Jack Welch's retirement.

Other times, CEO succession becomes an issue when a company is in trouble or is preparing for change. When Disney Corporation was in turmoil, for example, the company's longtime lead director sent an open letter to shareholders, announcing that the board of directors would begin more earnest discussions on succession candidates for CEO Michael Eisner.

It might sound as if Disney's Board was being proactive but, in fact, they were behind the curve. In January 2005, *BusinessWeek*'s "The Best and Worst Managers of the Year" feature listed Eisner among the worst. At the time, after dealing publicly with the question of succession for nearly a year, he still had only one legitimate internal candidate to replace him.

Ultimately, by choice (or maybe by necessity), the only internal candidate, Bob Iger, got the job. Contrast this to the example provided in Chapter 1, where GE had half a dozen executives primed to replace Welch. Disney had one. After Iger was named CEO, how many Disney executives left the company to become CEOs at other companies, as so many GE executives did after their new CEO was named?

Why would a company go all the way to the brink of such a major change without a plan for dealing with it? What would an investor think if a manufacturer treated its core raw materials that way, waiting until the last possible moment to source a critical supply, for example? Why don't more companies see talent management and, more specifically, succession planning as an opportunity to create value not just now, but for years to come?

Think of the value that businesses have reaped from analyzing, benchmarking, streamlining, and automating their supply chains for production materials and other business processes. The same is true of the talent supply. The only difference is that most companies have not yet figured it out.

The importance of succession planning at these levels is obvious, and Eisner's handling of Disney is an easy target. But again, it is not just executives. Succession planning for key positions, such as experienced corporate buyers, floor managers, engineers, cabinetmakers, account sales, accountants, and drivers is important to avoid devastating talent gaps and imbalances in a company.

Succession plans are a hot topic, and this issue will receive increased scrutiny. The Institutional Shareholder Services (ISS) now considers whether a company has a succession plan as a determining question in whether ISS will support proposed measures by public companies. As the ISS goes, so go many institutional shareholders who look to the ISS for an independent opinion.

## Turnover

Sometimes, rather than a single executive leaving the company, talent at one or more levels begins to leave, increasing the organization's turnover. Turnover is not necessarily a bad thing. Many companies experience good, productive, predictable turnover, which is necessary for a company's long-term growth. Procter & Gamble, for instance, has groomed executives internally, moved them up when the time is right, and seen shareholder value increase for years. GE, as shown earlier, follows a methodical approach for identifying and grooming its bench of executive talent.

Other companies, however, seem to turn executives over haphazardly. And analysts can tell the difference in the impact on the business. For example, Excite@Home, a former darling of the Internet world, experienced turnover at executive levels and eventually found itself bankrupt and searching for a buyer in 2001.

At the beginning of 2002, retail giant Kmart was facing bankruptcy after a period in which it appeared to burn through several high-profile executives and managers. The headlines of Kmart's press releases from March 1999 through January 2002 revealed extensive executive turnover at the company. Over that 35-month span, Kmart issued more than 40 announcements regarding executives moving in, out, or up, most describing multiple moves.

High turnover of great talent can be a problem that shareholders and business leaders should be concerned about and monitoring systematically. Analysts, shareholders, and company leaders would benefit from a more streamlined, transparent, and timely method of seeing turnover by having an opportunity to assess its impact in time to do something about it, if necessary. Ultimately, exposing executive turnover via standard reporting would allow stakeholders to find out whether the company's talent capital—and success—might be affected.

## Wrong Talent

Turnover can harm a business, but so can the wrong talent inside your organization that does not leave. All of the great recruiting, development, and management practices are meaningless if the raw materials in the supply chain are fundamentally flawed.

A successful talent plan and set of actions depend on the fact that you are hiring the best talent for the business, people with the right set of values and principles. During the "dotconomy" bust, the business landscape was littered with the broken shells of failed businesses with unseasoned, inexperienced management teams. These were examples of hiring at the right time but not the right talent. If these firms had been using talent metrics, could they have done a better job of hiring the right talent, thereby saving their businesses?

There is one example in this category that no businessperson will forget. It changed the way for the rest of us, and we continue to have to manage through the sins committed. Enron catalyzed an overhaul of the financial-reporting system in the United States. Enron did not sow the seeds of doubt about corporate leadership—it watered, fertilized, nurtured, and harvested them. The Enron case caused investors, shareholders, and regulators all over the world to sit up and take notice. The accounting industry will never be quite the same.

The "Enron scandal" could just as easily be called the "Arthur Andersen catastrophe." Arthur Andersen, the founder, started the firm decades ago on the principle that doing the right thing was more important than doing the easy thing. Arthur Andersen, the business, had long been known for resigning clients that it felt had questionable accounting ethics. The founder and his colleagues built a talent force that was respected and set industry standards. They thought of themselves as the best of the best, and they were great at sourcing the right talent and ensuring that they had the right talent in place for the future. But somewhere along the way, priorities shifted at Arthur Andersen, and they lost their footing.

In the 1990s, it is said that the firm hired executives who were more focused on growing the business than on maintaining the firm's standard of excellence. They allowed the talent brand to be compromised, and as a result, the culture shifted, becoming more oriented toward sales, billing, and revenue than toward the quality, objective work for which the firm had been known. The firm's audit practice became compromised by financial pressures from its lucrative consulting arm. The company was no longer willing to stand up to clients with substantial consulting revenues, fearing the loss of that money.

As a result of this shift in priorities, which had its roots in the company's executive talent base, the legacy that Arthur Andersen left behind will be images of paper shredding, lost retirement savings, and heightened regulation of the audit industry. Arthur Andersen will forever be associated with the catastrophic demise of one of the biggest U.S. corporations—and for allowing Enron to abuse its stewardship of vital public utilities at a cost to the American public that may never be fully understood. Arthur Andersen was a company that lost sight of its heritage, its culture, the things that made it successful, and ended up losing one of the most important assets for any company—its reputation.

How could Arthur Anderson have employed talent measurements, providing early indicators of a growing problem in the way the company's people were conducting business? Tracking the performance of new hires for their first 6 to 12 months (and then regularly thereafter) is one way for managers to identify and address issues early. Keep in mind that this method and others that occur post-hire might help you identify poor performers, but they will not save you from hiring the wrong talent in the first place.

Hiring right depends on your hiring managers understanding the organization's core principles, values, and make-up and hiring talent that reflect these factors. Ultimately, like it or not, we hire in the likeness of ourselves. We like people who are like us. It is human nature. We would rather surround ourselves with people that we like and can relate to than with those who differ from us. The culture of a company is most quickly changed by the talent that enters the door and the people who sway the hiring decisions. Stop and think about it—who are the "gate-keepers" for your organization?

Without performance metrics and active performance management, culture changes and performance degradation can sneak up on an organization as it might have at Arthur Anderson. One person who does not embody the company's values hires people in his or her likeness, and before long, the company is comprised of talent that no longer embodies the original core principles and values. That is a position no organization wants to find itself in.

Talent management technology will eventually allow companies to tie talent sourcing to the brand and messaging elements that attracted each candidate to the company. This is parallel to the tracking that companies do for product sales; applied to talent sourcing, it will help companies target their recruiting efforts in the areas that produce not the most candidates, but the highest-quality candidates who prove to be strong long-term contributors.

So far, rather than hearing much about company-driven metrics to proactively identify and solve talent-based problems, we have heard a lot about government oversight and regulation. Make no mistake; government oversight and regulation are certainly important, and the sanctions imposed on offending companies would be severe. But ultimately, it was the loss of reputation—damage to the brand images evoked by "Enron" and "Arthur Andersen"—that rendered those companies powerless to recover and doomed them for all time. Who would now be proud to have either of these companies on their resumé? Arthur Andersen's damaged reputation and credibility led to the subsequent loss of hundreds of clients around the globe who could no longer afford the risk of associating with the troubled auditor.

The consequences for Enron were similar. Even after Enron wrote down its revenues drastically, the company reported more than $800 million in 2000. It still had a company to run and talent to attract and retain. It still owned Portland General Electric, the Transwestern Pipeline Co., and the Northern Plains Natural Gas Co., among other companies. It had sizable assets that could have formed a healthy nucleus of operating revenue for a legitimately run energy firm. After the scandal broke, however, nobody wanted to do business with Enron, fearing it would either collapse or otherwise fail to fulfill its end of the deal.

Despite the company's asset portfolio, its credit rating was downgraded to junk status and its stock price fell to pennies. And Enron's talent— both good and bad—fled as fast as their customer base. You can imagine the uphill battle of trying to recruit anyone to either of these companies going forward. We will never know what the future would have held for Arthur Andersen. The crisis brought about its demise.

Since the collapse, some economists at the University of Washington and elsewhere have argued that the importance of reputation, credibility, and protecting the value of the brand was demonstrated so dramatically by Enron and Arthur Andersen that it will end up providing as much natural market incentive for companies to walk the "straight and narrow" as any new regulatory effort.

Perhaps regulatory efforts will point the way to new talent-force metrics. During the congressional hearings for the Corporate Responsibility Act, sponsors Senator Paul Sarbanes of Maryland and Congressman Michael G. Oxley of Ohio convinced the legislature that the SEC needs to examine what makes a good auditor, a good accountant, and a good board member. (In fact, they were deciding what makes up a good talent force.) When this was debated in Congress, some were asking, "Should we open up the windows or open up the door to the house?" If any one sentence sums up the attitude of the financial community after Enron, it was Sarbanes and Oxley's famous reply, "You should take the roof off."

Their point? The more visibility, the better. The more you can see inside a company and glimpse how it works and addresses its challenges, the better. All interested parties want to ensure that they have a handle on a company's leadership, talent base, culture, character, and future.

## Private Planning, Public Accountability

Beyond the benefits to individual business leaders, talent metrics are important to analysts, accountants, consultants, and investors, all of whom make at least a part of their living from understanding what makes one company different from another. Individuals in these roles, burned by Enron's smoke and mirrors, will find new ways to measure the true health of an organization. It will not be long before they also start looking at a company's talent management and talent capital for a reading on its organizational health.

The financial industry can fairly value just about any tangible or intangible business asset. Goodwill can be fairly estimated. Stock options are moving toward true valuation. All of these items appear on a company's financial statements.

How is talent measured and reflected on financial statements today? It isn't. Talent capital—the people and skills that a business brings to bear against challenges and opportunities—has become the last frontier for this kind of analysis and valuation.

More and more, cautious investors want to know about the leaders who are running a company—where they come from, how they manage, what makes them unique. Human resources executives are being asked to sit on the dais during shareholder meetings to address these issues. CEOs are being given talent-management objectives and asked to report on their progress—a solid precursor to more formal talent metrics.

European financial services conglomerate Allianz is one prime example of a company taking concrete steps to measure its talent practices. With 174,000 employees and 456 member companies worldwide,

Allianz is decentralized, but runs its talent management programs in a centralized fashion. The CEOs of each member company have broad latitude to run their businesses, and each one must report annually on his or her talent management practices, demonstrating measurable results.

Uniquely, Michael Diekmann, chairman of the board of Allianz, took over the group's HR function and still leads it in 2005. His overall position and that of the entire conglomerate is that if a member company does not have a solid talent management philosophy and methodology, then it does not have a sustainable business model.

Allianz is not alone in this belief. Companies all over the world that realize the competitive value of great people are starting to take concrete steps to measure how this talent affects the business. Progress in this area is seen in books, such as *The ROI of Human Capital: Measuring the Economic Value of Employee Performance* by Jac Fitz-Enz, the "father of human capital benchmarking and performance assessment" and founder and chairman of the Saratoga Institute, a PricewaterhouseCoopers service offering that helps organizations optimize their HR processes.

Analysts will find a way to estimate and identify the value that companies, such as Allianz, have brought to their bottom line through great recruiting and retention. These analysts are looking for numbers that consistently correlate to success—besides the number of gray hairs on the CEO's head. What is the value of one person versus another? What is the value of a strong human resources organization? What is the value of high retention rates or the kind of deep management bench that companies, such as GE, have developed? What numbers can practitioners use to measure effectiveness inside their own company?

Methods and measurements will be found to rate companies head-to-head in this arena. More and more, analysts and shareholders want to know what the company is doing to attract the best talent and what they are doing to retain and develop their employees. The inevitable breakthrough will represent new intellectual property for analysts, who make money from selling this information.

After one company's talent management and talent capital have been valued, it will not be long before they all are. Then, an entity, such as the Financial Accounting Standards Board, might look for a way to codify the value and create a talent-based asset in much the same way that goodwill rules quantify value for corporate brands and reputation. If that happens, the Securities and Exchange Commission might well start to ask for it as part of public company proxy statements.

Taking it a step further, corporate flameouts, such as we have seen with Kmart, could spur the next generation of the Sarbanes-Oxley Corporate Responsibility Act, requiring even more talent measurement. If solid, objective measurements can be found and agreed upon, Congress or the SEC could eventually mandate talent capital reporting as part of the proxy in the annual report.

Analysts and shareholders can already access the information to start identifying companies that have great talent management practices. Many early warning signs and red flags indicate talent-related problems, and these indicators are too obvious to ignore much longer. When this information is provided to broader audiences, by the time the annual proxy hits the Web or arrives in the mailbox, it will not be too late to act on the information. Sure, there are press releases and updates, but when was the last time you saw a press release announcing, "This is the second CFO we have turned over in the past nine months?"

The real value of great talent management is not on the compulsory, regulatory, compliance side. The real value comes when companies realize that talent measurement is one of the greatest business opportunities over the next decade and beyond. Why wouldn't a company want to use real data to improve in one of its most strategic areas?

Smart companies will quickly realize that they can improve today and create a competitive advantage that returns value to the company, or do nothing, get nothing, and quite possibly be forced to create these practices anyway through government regulation. If the same issue can either be an opportunity or a challenge for your business, why not take the opportunity and leave your competitors to grumble about the challenges?

| Rule 16B Officers | Chairman of Board | CEO | CFO | CAO | Chief Legal Counsel | Talent Officer | President | General Managers | Functional Executives |
|---|---|---|---|---|---|---|---|---|---|
| Name | | | | | | | | | |
| Title | | | | | | | | | |
| Time in Position/Dates | | | | | | | | | |
| Company Tenure | | | | | | | | | |
| Prior Person in Position/Dates | | | | | | | | | |
| Prior Person in Position/Dates | | | | | | | | | |
| % Turnover Past 5 Years | | | | | | | | | |

One simple measurement would be tying executives (public "Section 16B" positions) to tenure and turnover rates.

# Free Talent Zones—Using Talent to Drive Economic Development

All of this public interest in talent could have another intriguing side effect on economic stimulus programs. Nations and communities alike work hard to "sell" their locales to businesses. This phenomenon creates a chicken-or-the-egg question. Should state and local leaders follow the traditional path, working to lure businesses to their area and then counting on talent to show up? Or would it be more cost-effective, especially in smaller communities, to create incentives that lure talent to the region *first*, and then use that new community asset to attract businesses? Tackling economic incentives from the talent perspective might allow smaller communities to pull together existing people and resources and become more competitive in the hunt to attract business and jobs. And in the global economy, those jobs can come from just about anywhere.

Switzerland, long known for its creative tax-planning provisions, has made itself and some of its cantons (municipalities) attractive for multinational companies, some of whom have moved their European headquarters there. By providing the lowest corporate tax rates, Switzerland has brought thousands of new jobs into the country; many are filled by expatriates who bring in new currency for upgraded schools, new housing, and other beneficial projects. These companies provide new work and new jobs for the locals and add to the country's talent base, many who might never leave.

As another example, consider the community of Marquette, Kansas. This town of about 600 took a page from nineteenth-century home-steading programs, offering free land to folks for relocating there. As part of the program, Marquette divided 50 acres of farmland into 80 lots. As of February 2004, 21 of them had been given out, 20 of which went to newcomers. Four three-bedroom homes had been built, and construction was beginning on six more, with each home expected to add about $1,000 of tax revenue to the town's $350,000 annual budget. In a town with 127 school-age kids, six more had been added to the mix.

A similar program is in place in Paducah, Kentucky. The city's Artist Relocation Program provides a package of business, tax, financial, and cultural incentives in an effort to attract artists from across the United States into this formerly troubled spot between St. Louis and Nashville. The community gives artists the opportunity to buy affordable housing, along with gallery and studio space and other incentives. The program is breathing new life into Paducah, helping to attract visitors, expand the tax base, and increase property values. Perhaps, after all, there is some truth to the oft-quoted line from the movie *Field of Dreams*: "If you build it, they will come."

Could the same principles be utilized to attract doctors, teachers, and firefighters to a local community? Absolutely. It does not have to be land grants, although land is one area where smaller communities have an advantage. It could be tax incentives, college tuition assistance, even country club memberships—whatever works for the area and appeals to the talent it wants to attract. For example, loan repayment programs are already available for U.S. doctors who choose to relocate to certain underserved rural areas.

In November 2004, California voters approved Proposition 71, which provides unprecedented support for stem cell research. Freed from federal reluctance to provide stem cell lines or funding for the research, doctors in California will be in a much better position to make advances in this new science. *New York* magazine captured the broader potential talent market repercussions in its January 3, 2005, edition, under the headline "The California Stem-Cell Gold Rush: Will New York Lose Its Best Medical Minds to the Lure of Unfettered Research and the Promise of Biotech Billions?"

Doctors who have dedicated their lives to stem cell research elsewhere will now at least consider moving to California, where their work can enjoy much higher levels of investment and public support. Can it be long before a new ecosystem of stem cell biotech companies emerges in California? In this example, the state did not go out and woo companies to relocate in California, leaving the companies to recruit doctors and find investors. Instead, the state merely created an environment where all of those parties can come together and do the work they are all passionate about.

Another idea is to reach out to information workers, who are able to use technology to escape geographic boundaries. Could a consortium of writers and graphic designers be attracted to a small town in Georgia? If they were offered affordable housing, beautiful surroundings, and could continue to sell their services across the world via the Internet, then why not? Perhaps the community could start by upgrading its technology infrastructure, even offering Wi-Fi throughout the downtown area. The next step would be to launch an information campaign and invite the information workers to the town. Working together with the talent, the community could identify new ways to make the arrangement work.

This approach could also be used to help address some of the problems of offshoring discussed in Chapter 2. In rural America, for example, many towns have experienced unemployment rates of 9 or 10 percent.

These places have people ready to work. Presumably, it would also cost much less to run certain operations in, say, Moses Lake, Washington, than it would in San Francisco. In addition, the same technology that has enabled companies to use radiologists and call center workers from overseas can enable similar, domestic operations.

For companies, of course, decisions about where to locate often come down to cost. But offshoring is no panacea of free labor. It is a major expense, and many executives, when asked, say that if the costs were more competitive, they would much rather relocate jobs inside their home country than outside. Smaller communities are in a position to capitalize on that sentiment if they can make themselves more competitive.

To become even more competitive, what if the state of Washington and the city of Moses Lake took steps to lower those location costs even further? Perhaps they could develop a program, such as the one in Marquette or Paducah, to help subsidize worker salaries at a new plant in Moses Lake, exempting the workers from local property taxes, or even providing them with a lower state income tax. Maybe the state could help subsidize the employees' insurance and benefits costs.

Possibly, like Marquette and Paducah, communities will start looking for more creative ways to put themselves on the map. By using their ingenuity and resources, and by working together with talent, businesses, and state and federal government, communities where jobs are needed and the cost of living is lower might find that they can compete effectively in today's global talent market.

Not convinced that a real city could draw a viable talent base with the right incentives? For more proof, look no further than one of the fastest-growing city in the United States at the beginning of the twenty-first century. Decades ago, the city changed laws, rewrote rules, and designed and distributed incentives to create a city around an industry. Las Vegas was built to see whether they would come. And come they did, and they still do today—consumers, developers, financiers, knowledge workers, and working-class talent.

The idea of "free talent zones" is not so far-fetched. Are these our next competitive fields of dreams that communities should be taking a hard look at now to remain competitive?

# 7

# TALENT GOES
# ON OFFENSE

*Forces in Play: Like high-value free agents, Q-Talent can and will articulate its worth. Companies have the burden of putting up or losing out.*

In 1980, the oil industry drove a major portion of the U.S. economy and was a cornerstone for the emerging global business environment. As powerful and enormous as the industry was, however, many of its companies faced an Achilles heel: a talent shortage of quality, proven geologists—the people who, using technology, experience, wisdom, and a certain amount of chutzpah, made the recommendations about where to "punch the hole." Investors allocated millions of dollars and gained and lost fortunes based on the expertise of this industry-specific Q-Talent.

Soon, it became apparent to these geologists that they were not only crucial to the success of oil companies, but also that they were in short supply. Suddenly, recruiting them became much more difficult. Geologists with a track record began demanding "points," or a percentage of revenues from successful drilling sites. As time went on, the talent became more confident about its demands, asked for more, and often got it. Oil companies had to be creative and flexible to meet this new business challenge.

More recently, in India, a similar phenomenon is occurring with call center workers. Yes, those hourly, low-cost, call center workers. With offshoring en vogue, many companies have moved call center operations to India for a variety of reasons: Most educated people in India speak English, the education system is strong in many areas, technology systems and skills are advanced, and salaries in India are much more affordable than in North America or Europe.

But the explosion of offshore industry in India has created another high-demand situation for talent in some areas. As it turns out, only a few cities in India have the proper blend of people with English accents and education rates to effectively staff and run call centers. After they have been trained to perform efficient customer service for their parent companies abroad, a process that can be expensive for the parent company, these Indian business professionals are primed to be headhunted.

In some industries in India, annual turnover has approached 50 percent, exceeding most industrialized nations. The high demand for skilled talent in India is boosting wages at an annual rate of 30 percent, compared to less than 10 percent wage growth in the United States. To offset the new culture of job hopping and retain their valued call center talent, firms are implementing cultural changes, benefits improvements, bonuses, and other measures.

These two examples are separated by more than two decades and 10,000 miles, but the point they illustrate is the same—when candidates know they are valued and in short supply, they react by changing their behavior. Responding to such market conditions with more self-confidence and assertiveness is a side of human nature that transcends continents and cultures.

## The Talent Demand Cycle

What happened in the 1980 oil industry and what is happening today in India are not isolated phenomena constrained to specific roles or industries. With the convergence of trends described in Chapter 2, "Talent Market Demands"—generational shifts in the workforce, developments in the areas of immigration and offshoring, and emerging talent markets worldwide—certain companies and industries will begin to see their pools of available talent recede or evaporate. They will have more difficulty finding good talent for noncore positions and serious challenges retaining the Q-Talent that is so vital for any competitive business.

As the economy evolves, it leaves career holes in some places and creates career opportunities in others. Certain types of skills will become "commoditized," whereas others will become white-hot commodities. Some necessary skills might become rare as schools, colleges, and the culture focus on emerging information age careers. Other skill sets will be in high demand, forcing the talent pool to catch up. Even for companies that might not be in the proverbial skillet, there will still be a "trickle effect"—what happens when workers who possess high-demand skills are currently employed by *your* company?

If you find yourself managing a business or a department in this environment, you are not that different from the general manager of your favorite professional sports team, and you should start thinking more like the coach or head of player personnel. As with sports teams, acquiring Q-Talent is a continuous challenge for companies that want to be the best. They must always be thinking about landing superstars and keeping them. The quest for the best talent is not a spigot that you turn off when the yard is saturated.

We cannot predict where the next pinch will come from yet, but the cycle is predictable, and the demographic picture across the globe indicates that a change is coming. Do not be surprised if you are challenged by the next hot skill set in demand, even though you might feel like you are far away from the next booming industry. Change might be coming soon to the skill set in your industry, the talent employed in your business. It is important to get ahead and stay ahead by recognizing that candidates' and employees' new perspectives and behaviors represent another powerful force that savvy businesses need to understand and respond to now.

## Talent Knows: The Information Equation

How will these changes impact individual workers? As candidates begin to see increasing demand for their skills, their behavior will change. As more companies make talent a priority in their organization, as information technology makes communication even more convenient, and as the working population gradually shifts its priorities and values, each change will affect the psyche of individual workers.

The net effect will be a more empowered, more confident talent pool. Candidates will change the way they approach every facet of their working lives, from finding new opportunities, to negotiating for those opportunities, to thinking differently about their relationship to their jobs and organizations.

Thanks to the Internet and personal connectivity, people have access to an impossibly vast amount of information. Loads of detailed data are available about companies, their people, culture, and prognosis.

Much of this information is factual, coming in the form of analyst studies, media coverage, and the company's own statements. Other information is, shall we say, editorial in nature. All of it is mere seconds away. Candidates use this information to find jobs, apply for them, learn myriad facts about specific companies, and even dig up "dirt" about the companies through the electronic grapevine.

The sheer amount of information available and the ease of accessing it is changing the dynamics of how matches between companies and talent are made. Today, candidates know more, faster. They can search for interesting companies by industry, locale, and success factors, such as profitability or employee satisfaction. They use search engines, such as Yahoo! or Google, to find out more about the company and its industry. They can easily learn about the company's market, its opportunities, and how its products and services have fared and are expected to fare. And they can search for jobs all over the world.

Today, in only a few minutes, a candidate can Google key words, such as "proxy statement talent," and find hundreds of companies that say something about talent in their annual reports. In another few minutes, the candidate can dig a little deeper into those results. He can search for salary and benefits information using each company's name along with the key words "salary benefits."

Who has a stock-sharing plan? What about time off and Family Medical Leave Act benefits? Who is going to match the biggest share of employees' 401(k) contributions? If this is such a small company, why are they paying the CEO that much? Try it yourself. Experiment with different key words to find out about whatever job factors you believe are important. The information and access to it varies from company to company, industry to industry, and country to country. You can find all kinds of interesting information and usually determine, to some degree of satisfaction, which companies really seem to have their act together.

In addition to information provided by official sources, unofficial information is available, too. Many employees maintain blogs—increasingly popular and influential online journals and discussion forums—where job candidates can find out what people are saying about a company's executives, management style, and culture. Workplace rant forums, such as badbossology.com, wallyworldlife.com, and workingwounded.com, offer outlets for disenfranchised workers. These sites might contain internal company memos or e-mails, news articles, or written complaints from users. Some items on these sites are so juicy you have to pay for them.

---

**Blogs Bring Media Power to the Masses**

Initially viewed as little more than online diaries or journals, Web logs, or "blogs," are an increasingly influential form of communication. According to a November 2004 survey by the Pew Internet Project on the state of blogging in the United States, 27 percent of U.S. adult Internet users say they read blogs regularly, up from 17 percent just 9 months earlier. That represents a jump of 58 percent, to more than 32 million people.

Technorati, a search engine that tracks blog activity, claims that a new blog is created every 2.2 seconds. The number of blogs that Technorati tracks doubled every 5 months from June 2003 through March 2005. In South Korea, 75 percent of households have broadband access (compared to 20 percent in the United States) and blogging has exploded, with some estimates claiming that more than 20 percent of South Koreans maintain a blog.

Blogs are becoming major media players. The rising influence of blogs was driven home in 2004 during the American presidential campaign. On *60 Minutes II*, CBS News anchor Dan Rather reported about some documents detailing holes in President Bush's National Guard record. Before the broadcast was over, users of the conservative political blog FreeRepublic.com had posted questions about the documents' authenticity, pointing to fonts that appeared to have been made by modern word processors.

Soon, another blog, Power Line, linked itself to that conversation. Shortly after that, the Drudge Report, a site that reports news and aggregates news headlines from across the Internet (and is one of the most highly trafficked sites on the Internet), linked to the story on Power Line. What began as some whispers

---

on a conservative blog was now being discussed by millions of people around the world.

The next day, a headline on ZDNet, an online publisher of technology news, read, "Bloggers Drive Hoax Probe into Bush Memos." The *New York Times* wrote, "The debate over President Bush's National Guard service turned into a furious battle over the minutiae of Vietnam-era typewriter fonts on Friday." Later in the week, the *Los Angeles Times* wrote an enlightening dissection of the event under the headline, "No Disputing It: Blogs Are Major Players." "Rathergate," as it has been called, heralded the arrival of a new media power. Since then, Rather has stepped down, and CBS has fired others involved with the incident.

Proponents of blogging call it the democratization of the media, giving just about anyone the power to report major news events. Critics say that, absent a consistent ethic of fairness and balance, blogs cannot be trusted to accurately convey important stories.

In fact, just because the information is there does not mean it is true. There are those who say you will never win your battles in the public arena. And in today's age of bloggers, that saying is truer than ever. Some are now making it their mission in life to ensure that as many people as possible know what is on their mind. The *New York Times* recently gave these people a name: "determined detractors," those few who will try to sway the masses to their side. These people are now filling the Internet with their biases, often providing a heavy counterbalance to any good news. They each have their own motivations—sometimes a singular and personal cause, other times one backed by special interest groups and labor unions.

The bottom line? Blogs are another source of information that many find valuable, including job candidates searching for any piece of data they can find about the companies they are interested in.

Organizations that understand this new medium can use it effectively in their recruiting communications and employee relations programs. Companies that are caught unaware could find themselves caught up in the next big blog-driven headline.

Beyond these forums, just think of all the information sharing that goes on today through e-mail and instant messaging. How many jokes, observations, rants, and other comments do you get in your inbox every day? Any time a company issues a punitive memorandum, any time someone gets fired unfairly or insulted by a manager, you can be sure the relevant e-mails are shared among friends, family, and co-workers. If your company gets bad press, you can be sure those articles are being forwarded to and by your employees and posted on blog and chat sites. And, as always, you can be sure that all of those things are talked about in restaurants, at parties, and at the gym.

The Web, interpersonal connectivity, and an overall culture of information sharing among today's workers constitute a new, ad hoc Better Business Bureau for job seekers. With so many sources of job information, potential talent has unprecedented access to a raw, unfiltered, and potentially unflattering look inside a company. This kind of information is only going to become more prevalent and easier to find.

## Truth in Advertising Takes On a New Meaning

Employers unaware of this ongoing information exchange need to take notice. Organizations with a compelling brand, where the brand is consistently conveyed in how the company is perceived and talked about, are going to be the most attractive to Q-Talent that knows its worth and will not settle for less than the best.

A company's brand is no longer conveyed only by its Web site and other marketing channels, such as print or radio advertising. Although most companies understand the value of investing in these traditional areas, many still have not caught on to the ramifications posed by the broader Internet community, where information on just about everything is available all the time. With the information spigot turned on forever, the best thing a company can have going for it is the truth.

Thinking of buying a television? Punching the make and model number into the Google search engine will give you instant access to dozens of reviews, user comments, and prices. You can tell in a few minutes whether the TV you are considering performs well and what it should cost. As a result, the guy at Television Warehouse had better tell you the truth, or you will probably take your money elsewhere.

The same is true of employers. A person applying to become an assistant manager at her local Wal-Mart store, for example, might find many agreeable messages on the company's Web site. But does the company live up to those messages? Suppose our job seeker recalls reading something about Wal-Mart and unions in the local newspaper. Going back to Google, she might try to get a handle on outside perceptions of Wal-Mart's labor practices by entering a search query such as "Wal-Mart labor." And although Google's geographically influenced algorithms sometimes produce varying results, one of the first items to pop up during a long stretch of 2004–2005 was the unflattering headline, "New Report Details Wal-Mart Labor Abuses and Hidden Costs." The accompanying report detailed a range of alleged abuses committed by Wal-Mart upon its employees.

You can imagine the hair on the job seeker's neck standing up already. But that's not all. The announcement also links to a full report, which contains 20 pages of alleged abuses by the company, supported by 107 footnotes. Among the report's assertions:

- Sales clerks at Wal-Mart made $8.23 per hour on average in 2001, or $13,861 per year for those employed full-time. The official U.S. government poverty level for 2001 was $14,630 per year. In addition, employees work an average of 32 hours per week at Wal-Mart, not the 40 that is standard in the United States, meaning that the average Wal-Mart sales clerk took home less than $1,000 per month in 2001.

- Part-time employees must wait two years before they can enroll in the company's health-care plan. The industry average in the United States is 1.3 months. Wal-Mart classifies as "part-time" anyone working fewer than 34 hours per week, even though its workers average 32 hours per week. The company openly encourages employees to file for public health-care assistance, passing the cost along to taxpayers.

- Wal-Mart is the subject of a class action lawsuit brought on by more than *one million* former and current female employees alleging workplace discrimination.

- Thirty-nine more class action lawsuits, involving hundreds of thousands of current and former employees, have been brought against the company for alleged nonpayment or underpayment of wages, as employees were forced to work off the clock, or even had hours deleted from their timesheets.

Given the apparent disparity between Wal-Mart's public messages and its alleged behavior as portrayed on the blogs (although there are bloggers who also defend Wal-Mart) the question remains, will a candidate enthusiastically put their family's future and financial security in the company's hands?

Talent management practices that invite these types of Internet-driven information campaigns are simply not sustainable over the long term. These information campaigns might not have as much of an effect on the unskilled portion of Wal-Mart's workforce, but how will they affect the company's ability to bring in quality managers, buyers, and other critical roles? Sooner or later, the policies and the headlines they generate are going to create challenges for the world's largest company.

> **Note:** Wal-Mart has reacted to some of their negative press and has stepped up employee programs and worked hard to participate in community activities. For example, Wal-Mart provided financial and goods assistance for the Hurricane Katrina victims in New Orleans, Louisiana, and guaranteed that any displaced employees from the region would be guaranteed jobs in the interim once their affected stores are back up and running.

Wal-Mart is not alone. The biggest and the best-perceived organizations will all deal with similar challenges at one time or another. It is part of growing up and one of the fallouts of being in the public eye. If you are a leader, you will eventually be challenged and you can join the ranks of Microsoft, The Gap, Nike, Cintas, Starbucks, Fed-Ex, Electronic Arts, Home Depot, Wal-Mart, Fox, and others who have all been a target at one time or another and who, from that point forward, have had to factor the consequences into their talent brands.

> **Note:** The decision to change jobs can be one of the most important and stressful events in a person's life. Today,

with nearly unlimited company information—official and unofficial—immediately and easily accessible, more and more people are relying on it to guide their job search. Companies can increasingly count on talent to research job-related decisions more thoroughly. And the information that is available is not restricted to large companies. The low-cost platform of the Web means that medium-sized and small companies are profiled and discussed, too.

Try this: Take the perspective of a job candidate, go online, and see what information you can dig up about your current organization and your competitors. You might be surprised by what you find.

## The Importance of Your Virtual Lobby

Information is everywhere and is available at unprecedented rates, in unprecedented amounts. Candidates are armed with data that makes them more confident, savvy negotiators. As candidates find companies of interest, there is one more place they will look for information about those companies—the companies' own Web sites.

Candidates visit your Web site with expectations for how the site should look, what information it should contain, what actions they should be able to take, and how they should be treated. As discussed in Chapter 4, "The Cultural Obsession of Work," your talent brand needs to be properly expressed on your Web site because candidates' experience on your site will significantly impact how they perceive your organization and whether they would consider working there.

The good news is that organizations can completely control the face they put on their own Web presence. Companies often invest a great deal in their physical lobby and reception areas. It is an important way to show that they take pride in their appearance and convey a sense of professionalism. It is also often immediately apparent when a company has taken the same care in hiring and training the receptionists that greet visitors.

A company's Web site is its new lobby, and the impression it makes is every bit as important as its physical lobby to the company's ability to compete. Companies must become more strategic in looking at and measuring the value that their Web presence brings to their recruiting efforts.

Savvy organizations of all sizes have finely crafted Web sites that serve customers' needs. Their Web site copy is targeted, tweaked, and massaged. A range of helpful services are provided for customers, journalists, and others to find information about the company. They might have focused intense resources on the problems of getting ahead of demand when it comes to their supply chain, production processes, and other aspects of the business. Slick designs add to the visual appeal. All of these steps are necessary and good.

But overall, companies have not taken the same strategic steps when it comes to their most important competitive asset—their talent. Too often, companies have slapped together some employment-related copy and posted it on the Web just to have something there.

As we reviewed in depth in Chapter 5, "Building a Talent Community," by using technology that is available today, companies can retool their employment Web pages to automatically capture information, build relationships with candidates, and provide candidates with information of interest while automatically qualifying them for an opportunity.

---

**A Gracious and Inviting Employment Web Site**

The employment area of a company's Web site serves as receptionist, recruiter, and virtual lobby for potential talent. Therefore, just as they do with their physical lobby, companies should strive to make their Web site a welcoming place for potential talent as well as customers, with a look and feel that captures the brand of the overall company and its culture. Here are some ways your Web site can provide talent with a taste of what it might be like to work for you:

- **Welcoming messages.** Ideally, these should come from someone important in the company. Imagine that you got to meet the CEO, functional vice president, or a department leader the minute you walked into a company's lobby. That is the effect you are looking for in your greeting.

---

- **Easy access.** There should be a link to your main employment page from your company's home page. People need to be able to access the employment pages in as few clicks as possible. Imagine having to circle a company's building looking for the main entrance, only to end up standing outside the door, waiting to get inside. It sounds simple, but it is amazing how many companies get this wrong. "Easy entrance, quickly accomplished" is the mantra.

- **Exploring opportunities.** Help the candidate answer his or her own questions about the company. If the company's facilities are a selling point, you might provide a virtual tour. If benefits are a strength, offer a look at them.

- **Assurances.** Make sure candidates know that their time has not been wasted. If candidates fill out a registration form or request information, the site should promptly reply with a message that reinforces the interaction and thanks them for their time.

As the need for talent increases and companies find themselves competing for the best available talent, well-planned sites that deliver real value to the company *and* the candidate will become more prevalent. Smart companies will begin working on this today. For others, the changes will come after they start hearing about where they fall short in this area during interviews and in e-mails and letters. Why does your site only accept resumés? Why did it take you weeks or months to respond? Why do I have to give you my name and phone number when I just want to find out more about your company? Your competitor has a unique way of dealing with me on my terms; why don't you?

Companies need to learn how to use the Web in the ways described in Chapter 5 so that their sites invite participation and return value to all parties. Using the Web to build relationships across the recruiting spectrum—with everyone from passive candidates to active job seekers—is a critical competency for companies that want to hire Q-Talent at a time when talent is more empowered than ever.

The Internet offers a wealth of information to help candidates determine their market value. Here, Payscale.com serves up expected benefits and compensation for a sous chef.

## The New Interview

Whether it is provided on your company's Web site or someone else's, one of the nuggets in the steady stream of job-related information is data about a candidate's value in the marketplace, including expected compensation and benefits. Understanding that knowledge is power, some companies have long resisted publishing salary figures and specific benefits information. But today, anyone can easily find out the market value of an accountant, underwater welder, or aeronautical engineer and what benefits such a position should provide. Just "Googling" any job title coupled with the word "salary" will often provide useful results. Sites like Salary.com and Payscale.com provide a wealth of this type of information.

In some ways, this newfound access to compensation data shifts some burden to the job seeker. Hiring managers used to be amazed when a candidate walked in well prepared and it was clear that the candidate had done his homework. Today, there is no excuse for a candidate to show up for a job interview unprepared.

---

### A Cautionary Tale

Just as companies can be negatively impacted by unsavory details shared about them via the Web, e-mail, and other means, individuals can also be "bitten" by broad information access. For example, some employees have embraced blogs as a forum where they "rant" about their companies and work experiences. Although these bloggers provide job candidates with a unique perspective about their workplaces, some have been fired as a result of their indiscretion. There is even a term for getting fired due to your blog—*dooced*—derived from Dooce.com, one of the first blogs to lead its owner to this fate.

By early 2005, Google, Delta Airlines, and the *Houston Chronicle* in the United States, and Waterstone's, a bookstore chain in Scotland, were among the companies that had fired employees due to their work-related blogs. In February 2005, an individual in Iran was charged with "spying and aiding foreign counter-revolutionaries" after criticizing the arrest of other online journalists on his blog. He received a 14-year jail sentence.

A graduate school admissions incident provides another cautionary tale. In March 2005, an individual posted information online telling business school applicants how to view their admissions status prior to receiving official notice from the schools in question: Harvard Business School, MIT's Sloan School of Management, Stanford's Graduate School of Business, Duke's Fuqua School of Business, Carnegie Mellon's Tepper School of Business, and Dartmouth's Tuck School of Business. A nice "win" for the applicants, right? Wrong. The schools were able to track which individuals breached their systems.

Each school responded differently. Stanford reviewed these individuals' applications on a case-by-case basis. Harvard Business School provided the most immediate and extreme response; its dean, Kim Clark, told the *Boston Globe*, "We expect our applicants to be personally responsible for the access to the Web site, and for the identification and passwords they receive." Harvard rejected all 119 applicants who prematurely accessed their admissions site.

The electronic medium makes certain activities so easy, they seem innocuous—complaining about your boss, accessing restricted information, and so on. However, this ease of use does not mean you should abandon good judgment and engage in activities online that you would be more careful about, if not avoid entirely, in an offline setting. The same "offline" rules about good judgment apply online. Think before you act. Your employment—or future employment prospects—might be at stake.

However, most consequences for job seekers are overwhelmingly positive. With this newfound wealth of compensation-related information, an accountant, zoologist, marketing professional, or dental hygienist now walks into an interview with more of an edge. The hiring authority used to ask the loaded question, "What are you looking to make?" Today, a skilled accountant, who has this information in her back pocket, can merely hit the ball back into the employer's court—"This looks like a good company, and I'm sure you'll make me a competitive offer that is in line with or better than the market rate for someone of my education, experience, and talent." The candidate may even be thinking, "And by the way, I have the spreadsheet in my briefcase if I need to pull it out for you . . . which you don't want me to do."

In any industry that experiences a skills shortage, you can expect candidates to become even bolder in their demands. (Remember the oil geologists?) Candidates might have specific information about who is managing the division or department and insist on meeting with that person. They might not even want to talk to someone who is not directly connected to the hiring authority. Why waste time meeting with someone who cannot make something happen? They might have seen organization charts and have questions about them. They might see that their prospective boss, the director of marketing, reports to the CFO or some other unfavorable proposition and not bother to inquire about the job in the first place. They might have heard about an unusual compensation arrangement and ask to explore it.

The candidates who take the time to do extensive research are more likely to be the Q-Talent that companies need. These candidates also present some new wrinkles for those doing the hiring. The interview is now starting to look more like a sales meeting, with the candidate a valued client and more important decision makers at the table, people who can accurately and compellingly tell the company's story. If the right decision makers are not at the table, the candidate might ask for them to be. The candidate's knowledge of her worth in the marketplace leaves her holding more of the cards, and her negotiating skills may markedly improve.

It is incumbent on companies facing this more informed, savvy candidate to do their own homework about standard market values for the positions they are offering, typical benefits, and even which perks the competition offers. When a candidate asks for more information or for time with additional employees—even executives—smart companies will make every reasonable effort to comply. Companies must approach their end of job interviews and negotiations in a professional and well-planned way and extend the best possible offer.

When candidates join your company, they approach their employment status differently than previous generations did during the days of "lifetime employment" and intense job loyalty. Your employees are saturated with information about careers and the job market in the ways described in Chapter 4. Those with exceptional skills or accomplishments—the Q-Talent you especially want to retain—might be approached by employees or recruiters from other firms, either formally or informally, regarding opportunities.

Using the Internet, employees can easily stay up-to-date on their market value and might inform their manager if their compensation falls behind market norms. These employees are now the ones maintaining blogs, sending e-mail, and instant messaging their friends and colleagues about their jobs, projects, colleagues, managers, and companies. What will they say about working for your organization? We take a closer look at retention in the next chapter.

Information accessibility and a competitive labor market combine to give new advantages to Q-Talent and provide new challenges for companies seeking to acquire and retain the best people. The resulting dynamic in job searches and job interviews might not quite approach the free-agency phenomenon in professional sports, but in some industries, such as transportation, agriculture, medicine, and technology, it might get close.

# 8

# RELATIONSHIP RECRUITING (STILL) RULES

---

*Forces in Play:* Even with an online talent community of millions, relationship recruiting remains a competitive advantage and differentiator. Talent must have a name and a face for you to win them over. Continuous recruitment is required not only to attract the next generation of Q-Talent, but also to retain your existing Q-Talent.

---

Imagine the following scenario: You are interviewing a candidate for an executive-level position in your organization. He supplied all the right answers to the initial screening questions. He is interested enough in your company to fly across three states for the interview. But now, as the interview draws to an end, he seems hesitant. He asks a couple good questions, but you cannot shake the impression that he is not sold on the role. Because of his hesitation, you are leaning toward a "no hire" recommendation. After the candidate leaves your office, you call the recruiter to discuss your impressions.

Having followed the candidate through the process, the recruiter listens to your feedback and has an immediate response. Your observation that the candidate is hesitant is correct, he tells you—but not for the job-related reasons you might suspect. In fact, the recruiter informs you, the candidate is concerned about high school athletic programs in your area. He wants the job. He wants it badly. But back at home, he has something else to be concerned about. His daughter is an all-conference basketball player. The team is counting on her. Basketball is her passion. He needs to be able to tell her that the program in your area is as good as, or better than, the one she is in now.

For this candidate, the toughest discussion in the entire interview process will happen around the family dinner table, not your conference table. His most difficult decision is not about whether to take the job, but about moving his daughter out of her basketball league.

Understanding the candidate's concerns, the recruiter can guide you and the entire interview team into an open discussion of this hurdle. The recruiter might connect the candidate with local high school basketball coaches so that he can talk with them directly about how his daughter's passion might translate to the new surroundings. In this instance, one of the recruiter's key roles is ensuring that the candidate has all the information he needs to effectively balance his desire for the job with his family considerations and to communicate this information to the interview team so they can make a fully informed hiring decision.

There is no technology perceptive enough, sensitive enough, or wise enough to navigate this kind of complex human situation. No matter how rapidly the world changes, no matter which trends affect the talent market, and no matter how technology advances our capabilities, the human dimension of recruiting will always be a major factor in a company's ability to attract and secure Q-Talent.

As discussed in Chapter 5, "Building a Talent Community," one of the most important roles that technology plays is automating some of the functions that your employees or contract recruiters have been performing, such as initial candidate screening. If you are using the Web functionality described in Chapter 5, you are delivering a stream of interested, qualified, and available candidates to the desktops of your recruiters and decision makers. The technology is automatically screening out a high percentage of unqualified individuals.

With this automatic filtering and your growing talent community in place, your recruiters no longer have to do an initial resumé review or make all of those screening phone calls or find every single applicant themselves. They are free, or at least a lot freer than they were before.

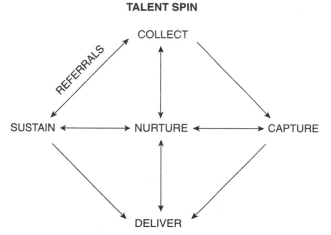

**TALENT SPIN**

The Web site can collect, capture, and even nurture your talent relationships,
but it takes a human approach to deliver the right candidate into your
organization and sustain those relationships over time.

So what does the talent organization do with all this newfound free time? They build relationships. Face-to-face relationships with both candidates and internal decision makers bring a higher level of sophistication and value to the recruiting process. Let's look more closely at how much value these face-to-face relationships deliver.

## The Human Touchpoint

We have talked about extending the product-marketing mindset to the recruitment process by using a disciplined approach to capture and communicate the heart and mind of your organization via a talent brand and corresponding messages. After you have established your online talent community, the processes of "collecting" and "capturing" never stop. The "talent spin" is a never-ending cycle.

But for all the benefits that technology can deliver, the final piece of the "talent spin" cannot be completed with technology. The "deliver" stage of the cycle requires the human element, where real people get involved to make decisions, solve problems, communicate, and build individual relationships.

Only a person can effectively develop and advertise the company's employment brand. Only a person, a skilled relationship recruiter, can look into people's eyes, shake their hands, ask them questions, and formulate a rich, nuanced, social understanding of each unique answer. In short, only a person can understand the needs of all parties in the hiring equation and deliver the right talent into the organization in the right place, at the right time.

The core of your efforts to attract and acquire Q-Talent is the basic understanding that people are not computers or advertising space or used cars. A computer can be sold to a company, but in the end, the computer does not have to decide to go there. The computer does not have to move its family or leave old friends. Computers do not worry about the risk involved. In business, it is easy to temporarily focus on metrics and spreadsheets, but the essential human element of business in general, and recruiting in particular, is just as potent as any number and often, much more so.

Numbers did not create the world of business. People did. And recruitment is an area of business that numbers cannot completely explain. Recruiting is a complex, bidirectional, *human* process. Recruiters need to understand and manage a complex social matrix consisting of the candidate, all of her influencers, the company, the hiring manager, the departmental players, and often many others.

Furthermore, technology or no technology, you are not going to hire somebody sight unseen. Does the person fit with the group? Is the chemistry there? "Fit" cannot be assessed any other way than through face-to-face interaction.

At some point, if she passes all the preliminary screening, the candidate will meet her potential peers, supervisors, and other influencers inside the company. These people make a hiring decision based on their interactions with the candidate, the most crucial juncture of the entire process. At this stage, the recruiter plays a pivotal role. As previously discussed, the recruiter needs to have a thorough understanding of the company, its goals, industry, culture, and the qualities that a candidate needs to possess to get the job. The recruiter knows the key influencers and is in tune with the desires of the candidate. Overall, good recruiters have a high "EQ," or emotional quotient—a high level of intelligence and sophistication when it comes to human nature.

Throughout the process, the recruiter is on the "front line" of the interviews, orchestrating, so that all goes smoothly and so that all the necessary information is available for the candidate and interview team to make well-informed decisions. The recruiter needs to be in tune with everybody's needs, desires, hurdles, and concerns. The hiring process elicits emotions, gut reactions, and assumptions that can have a direct, sometimes adverse, effect on decision-making. The recruiter uses his skillfulness to uncover whether any of those forces are at play, ferret out the necessary information, help everyone come to the most informed conclusion, and ultimately deliver the right candidate to the organization.

This front-line role is as critical as the person who you send to Wall Street to build analyst confidence in the state of your business. Although not as public, the stakes are just as high. The one great talent that gets away is like the one new institutional shareholder who decides not to buy into your stock. It is a loss that can magnify itself. It is a loss that might never be fully understood or quantified.

How can you put a dollar figure on the importance of this competency to the company? Do you value your top salesperson? How about the recruiter who has brought in three of your top five salespeople? Who has delivered more value to the company? Are the people who currently recruit for your company bringing in the kind of value they should be?

Although these concepts may sound basic, in practice they are extraordinarily complex. The recruiter provides alignment among the organization, the department, the position being filled, and all of the people involved along the way. The recruiter needs to synthesize all of these people and the related business issues for the company to get the most out of its hiring process and the best Q-Talent into its open positions.

---

**Ten Qualities of Great Recruiters**

Recruiting Q-Talent requires hard work, knowledge, wisdom, strategy, and, at times, a little bit of luck. Recruiters must understand a broad range of issues across the cultures, teams, and industries they work with, as well as the nuts and bolts of what drives each unique individual candidate. It is a highly skilled profession, requiring someone who can master mostly intangible factors to bring about tangible results—the best hire for each and every open position.

Great recruiters . . .

- Love to learn, digging in to whatever part of the business they represent.

- Meet new people at every opportunity.

- Are adventurous . . . see themselves as the Indiana Jones of recruitment.

- Thrive on competition and winning.

- Work happily in the background and do not require pats on the back.

---

- Seek solutions, believing answers can be found and tasks completed when others may have given up.

- Practice strategic consultative selling, closing two parties at the same time, every time.

- Think strategically, stay a step ahead, and come prepared with a contingency plan.

- Enjoy project work and starting fresh every day.

- Believe they have the best job on earth.

## The Evangelist Culture

There is an old joke about souls being recruited to Heaven and Hell. They take a trip through Hell and see a world of golf courses, casinos, happy hour every day at 5 o'clock, and many of them sign up. The next day, when they report to Hell, they are immediately cast into a lake of fire to spend eternity. "What gives?" they say. "This isn't what we saw yesterday."

"That's because," says the devil, "yesterday, you were a recruit."

You might be thinking by now that this is not a book about retention.

But then again, maybe it is.

Recruiters are not the only human touchpoint in the process of finding and acquiring great talent. Your employees are powerful touchpoints, too. This constituency often gets overlooked or taken for granted. Employees are the most critical, most immediate talent community, and companies are constantly building (or destroying) relationships with this community.

If companies make talent a priority and work hard to hire the best Q-Talent available, they must work equally hard to retain that talent, or all of those initial efforts go to waste. For the purposes of this book, recruiting and retention cannot be separated from one another. Attracting and retaining are symbiotic activities. To retain the best people, business leaders should be thinking about recruiting their own talent every day.

Why? For one thing, if you are not continuously recruiting your best employees, nurturing relationships of value with them as you do with external Q-Talent, then guess what—your competitors are. Do not waste time fighting over internal Q-Talent (for example, by restricting great employees from pursuing compelling opportunities elsewhere in the organization). Although some restrictions on internal transfers are legitimate for relatively short-term business reasons, long term, it is in the company's best interest to allow Q-Talent to move around to pursue a career path, stay invigorated, and make your organization a vital place where Q-Talent can grow.

Additionally, think of all of those recruiting messages, all those great things you told your potential talent to sell the employment experience at your company. If those things are not true in practice, they will come around and bite you on the retention side. In the end, you might build great recruiting processes, only to find yourself pouring water into a leaky bucket. Internal practices that do not match up with the "face" of a company's recruiting messages will cause the same frustration and resulting damage to the talent brand as poor recruiting.

When companies do not recruit to the truth, new employees recognize it and feel immediate resentment. Over the long term, "bait and switch" recruiting practices will damage your ability to attract and retain Q-Talent.

Remember, news about a company's culture is shared on the Internet and spreads fast. Recruiting efforts that are not honest, respectful, and gracious can easily create dissatisfaction, even bitterness, and those feelings can last—and multiply. Now the company has two problems: a disgruntled employee who is sharing his resentful feelings both inside and outside the company and, eventually, an opening to fill again. Only it gets harder to fill that spot the second or third or fourth time around. This is a bad cycle for the company.

When does recruiting stop and retention begin? The answer is largely semantics. Before the offer is made, before it is even accepted, the company should be thinking about keeping its new talent. Expect your quality candidate to receive a counteroffer. Expect doubts and anxieties to surface. Expect him to have to answer hard questions from his personal influencers, such as family members or friends. It is a good thing you have staffed your talent organization with savvy people who understand the needs and priorities of all parties and know how to address them openly, truthfully, and graciously.

Chances are, you have already got a lot of great talent in your organization. Keeping these people happy is imperative not only to operational success, but also to the success of your talent recruiting strategy. Referrals from current employees often account for 30 percent to 40 percent of a company's new hires. Recruiters cannot afford for companies to disenfranchise a resource like that.

Interestingly, this 30 percent to 40 percent of referrals typically comes from a small percentage of employees. When starting a company, most people surround themselves with friends and family, the people they trust the most. When working for a company, however, most people have a hard time referring friends and family to work there. Doing so is an emotional, risky proposition. But there are many things these employees feel comfortable doing that can help spread the word about your company. It could be as simple as having your talent Web site URL and its tagline printed on the back of the company's business cards. It could be posting flyers at the local university. It could be introducing someone to a recruiter via e-mail.

For those who do refer candidates, the talent organization should take steps to identify who is referring the best and approach those people to see whether they can recommend others for future job openings. In addition, asking for referrals immediately upon the conclusion of the hiring process can often increase the response rate. New employees are excited about their decision to join your company and are looking for validation from the company, family, and friends. Providing a referral and getting affirmation from a friend they introduce to this great new company feeds their excitement and need for validation. Asking early for referrals from new hires works.

In addition to referrals and some of the other simple steps just described, one of the most powerful assets (or liabilities) in your recruiting arsenal is simply the way in which employees talk about their jobs. This is impossible to control completely, but the company can do many things to ensure that this employee "chatter" helps its recruiting efforts. Does every employee understand the company's mission, goals, culture, and values? More important, are those values true and relevant to your employees? If someone asks one of your employees about your company, would his response reflect the image and philosophy of the company in the most accurate and persuasive light? If a group of employees takes a job candidate to lunch and the candidate asks, "What is the company's culture like?" would the response be consistent and positive?

Most companies have a mission statement and a codified set of core values. In case you have forgotten why you created those in the first place, here is a big reason: You want your employees to unify around those concepts, not only to achieve business goals, but also to accept and internalize your mission, values, culture, and everything these factors represent about what is great about being part of the company. If the mission statement and company values are relevant and true to your current employees, they can be a tremendous asset for recruiting. If employees are satisfied and deeply grounded in the company's mission, philosophy, and culture, the "face" that candidates see will validate the corporate values and reinforce the messages being communicated through the company's Web site. The candidate will begin to feel the sense of trust that comes from experiencing consistent behavior over time.

On the other hand, if the company recruits with false promises—if the company's value statements and brand image communicate one story, but its employees experience something different—what do you suppose the conversations between candidates and employees sound like? As previously discussed, those conversations, happening online and offline, can add up quickly in the digital age. The cumulative effect of any negative word-of-mouth can become a deep, devastating liability to the talent equation. Your company might never even find out that this "side conversation" is happening. Companies must continually work to ensure that they do not create this kind of adversity for themselves. And it begins on the inside.

Companies that do this right are easy to spot. Southwest Airlines, whose employees have been profiled on a cable television reality show, A&E's *Airline*, is one example. Southwest's employees enjoy the latitude to inject personality, spontaneity, and enthusiasm into their work, knowing it is part of the company's brand and understanding the acceptable parameters for their behavior. This helps them to be calm, confident, and empowered in their work. Their attitude, in turn, supports and reinforces Southwest's brand identity. Over time, this consistency transforms into long-lasting goodwill among customers as well as potential talent. The interplay of these forces creates positive momentum that only grows. It is no coincidence that Southwest is consistently rated one of the top companies to work for.

Furthermore, viewers of the A&E show are exposed to the different positions at SWA. They see how employees are empowered, the stress they go through, and the rewards they enjoy. It is a reality show, but at its heart, it is an employment brand exercise that defines and reinforces the SWA culture. In this way, candidates who come to SWA have a good idea of what to expect and, as long as these expectations match their experiences as employees, SWA will continue to reap the benefits.

Your company might never have its own reality television show, but a properly positioned, truthful, well-communicated talent brand can bring the same kind of lasting value that builds over time, whether your company is an international monolith or a small, neighborhood landmark.

Chapter 4, "The Cultural Obsession of Work," discussed the importance of a talent brand as a way to communicate with potential stars who are just beginning to learn about the company. Here, the talent brand comes full circle. If your talent brand messages are more than just words, employees know it. If those messages are true, your employees feel it. And when they meet potential new talent, they will show it.

## Succession, Development, and Planting the Seed

Previous chapters discussed the importance of succession planning and talent management plans. Although these steps are critical for the executive segment, companies also stand to gain tremendous value, both in terms of economics and employee satisfaction, by extending those efforts all the way down the line.

No matter how great your recruiting practices, keeping quality people will always be easier, cheaper, and more productive than finding new ones. Yet if most companies hold up the mirror and look at the programs and processes they have in place, they will likely find that their retention efforts, like their former recruitment practices, are based on the same old "arrogance of supply."

From a purely bottom-line standpoint, even with all of the efficiency gains and cost reductions that companies can achieve through great recruiting practices, there will always be a "cost to hire." From a productivity standpoint, an open position is an open position, whether it is caused by inefficient recruiting or a lack of great retention programs.

The economic benefit of retention can be illustrated with a fact most often delivered in a marketing context: The cost to acquire is higher than the cost to retain. For example, if an Internet service provider has to spend $100 in advertising, promotions, customer service, and internal processes for each new subscriber, then at $9.95 per month, the company needs to keep each subscriber for a year or more to make that investment worthwhile. However, the second year they retain the same subscriber is pure gravy, and as long as the company continues to provide good service, there is less reason for the subscriber to leave.

The situation is similar with talent. If a department head leaves, it will cost you something to replace him. Regardless of whether you have efficient processes, great recruiters, and a super candidate-management system, there is always a cost to hire.

Furthermore, if the company looks externally to replace the department head, chances are fairly good that the external talent will cost a little bit more. Now you have got a cost to hire, a period of lower productivity as the new person is trained, and a higher salary figure to boot. In this way, turnover can add up quickly in a real, economic sense.

With retention, development, and succession, companies have a solid way to keep a handle on those costs. By promoting an employee into the department head role, the company might realize a small reduction in salary, zero cost to hire, and much less lag time in bringing the person up to speed. These efficiencies can be repeated in moving another employee into the position vacated by the person who took the department head job, and again on down the line to the entry level. In this scenario, everybody moves up, takes on more responsibility, gets a raise—and the company's costs actually go down. Everyone wins.

Promoting from the inside also allows companies to more selectively decide where to bring people in from the outside. For example, promoting or even laterally transferring a salesperson who is ready for new challenges might allow the company to then hire a great salesman they have wanted on the team. This approach helps keep employees engaged and fresh, brings their ideas to new areas of the company, and provides them with more opportunities to learn and grow along the way.

The employee satisfaction element might seem self-evident: If people have a career path, they are more likely to stay and see it through. If you feature career development programs in your recruiting messages, make sure new employees see evidence of those programs soon after they are hired.

## The First Face to Face

With "high EQ" recruiters and employees who are aligned with the company's goals and values, you are ready to bring in talent for the first "face to face." As discussed in Chapter 5, the company's careers Web site should be designed so that it invites and then nurtures a relationship with everyone who walks into its virtual "lobby." Its messages should align with the company's in a way that taps into the inner motivations of each participant. It should provide useful information, product and services discounts, and other valuable content, in the format and at the intervals of the participant's choosing.

As previously discussed, all of these efforts and strategies are building toward the day when the right opportunity comes along and the company asks its interested, qualified, and available talent-community participants to express their interest and, for those who qualify, show up in the flesh.

These candidates have visited the company's career site, joined the talent community, answered qualifying questions, and have been identified by the company as desirable talent. They might have been receiving information and communications from the company for weeks, months, or even years. If your messages have been consistent, interesting, and valuable, the candidates might even feel like they know you. They certainly will have expectations based on all they have seen and heard about you.

At this point, the consistency between the company's messages and its behavior is put to the test. Remember, hiring is a bidirectional process. As discussed in Chapter 7, "Talent Goes on Offense," the candidate is screening the company as much as she is being screened.

One of the foremost questions in her mind is, "What would it be like to work here?" She wants to know whether it is as good as it seems or whether all that talent-community stuff was just a mirage. She might actually come out and ask the questions, "What is your culture truly like? Do you enjoy working here? Why?"

Again, these questions, this moment, is why it is so important for the employment experience to match the experience conveyed by the recruiting and branding messages. If employees have been treated inconsistently, if the company has failed to follow through on its promises, or if its messages simply do not match reality, employees will hesitate before they answer. They might look at each other and smile, roll their eyes, adjust their glasses before responding. When they do respond, their voices might contain a hint of cynicism or sarcasm.

These warning flags, however subtle, might not be a make-or-break issue for the candidate, but they can certainly make a difference. A negative or confused response might raise questions in her mind: "What did that answer really mean? Are they hiding something? Do I really want to be here?" The position might be perfect for her, but if she has doubts about the company, her decision about whether to work there will be much more difficult.

This is why it is crucial to constantly reach out to your own employees, to constantly recruit your own. When candidates ask your employees these questions, there should be consensus and affirmation. If the candidate asks three people those same questions—what is the company like, do they enjoy working there—and gets an immediate response that says, "This is how we have defined our culture, these are the things that we do to put our culture into practice, and this it what it means to me," that, too, stands for something. In fact, it means a great deal to most people to find out that what they have heard about a company matches the experience of those who work there. It generates excitement about the prospect of making a change. Your open position might not be ideal for her, but her positive impression of the culture may be enough to swing her decision in your favor.

There are other benefits to involving employees in the hiring process. Employees might feel privileged to participate in this important process. They might feel more valued by the company. And the mere act of expressing the positive aspects of the company can have a rejuvenating effect on them. The chance to sell the company and talk about their work in a positive way to someone who really wants to listen can be an invigorating experience that keeps employees refreshed, recommitted, and recruiting all the time.

## Continuous Improvement: The Key to a Lasting Competitive Advantage

The cyclic nature of the talent community helps you continuously attract, capture, and deliver great talent to your organization. In the midst of this never-ending cycle, how do you stop long enough to find out whether you are being effective? How do you find out whether people perceive that their interactions are consistent with the company's brand? How do you know whether the messages and the image you are spinning in your talent Web are compelling? If so much of the talent brand reputation is established "underground," how can a company bring this reputation to light?

Part of the answer lies in the talent plan discussed in Chapter 3, "Building a Competitive Talent Organization," and the talent metrics described in Chapter 6, "Tangible Talent Measurement." Each company may have unique ways of measuring its success, but the ability to put some kind of measure on progress is a critical component of any talent plan. You should be measuring how quickly the company is filling its openings and whether the talent/succession plan has worked as it should. You should know how the company's bench strength has changed over time and what the company's internal and external talent "inventory" looks like. The mere act of creating and reporting on your talent plan will provide many good indicators of your progress.

Another important way to get a reading on your recruiting effectiveness is to take another page from the traditional marketing playbook and simply ask lots of people—listen and learn. Remember, you now have a community of prospective talent interacting with the company on a regular basis. Ask them what is working and what is not. Send them a link to an automated survey that they can complete on your Web site. Make it as easy as possible and offer something in return for their participation.

For candidates who make it to the interview process, ask them to fill out a survey with questions about their experience or to at least debrief with the recruiter to share information about their experience.

Ask your employees, too, getting their feedback via open dialogue, anonymous surveys, and so on—whatever approach best fits your culture. Ask someone who has recently been hired and someone who rejected your job offer. Find someone who has recently left the company and hold an exit interview to dig deep into things that person would change about your company's culture. Do not be surprised if you hear the same manager's name more than once. Do not be offended if the person does not like the company. But do find out why.

Regardless of whom you approach, start with four simple words: "We need your help." Explain honestly that the programs in question are new, the talent community is new, and the company needs help to understand how it can improve itself. Did the recruiting experience match the person's expectations? Was it timely and informative? What would they change about the interview process or, for employees, about working at the company? Each person's experience will be unique. What you need to find are the common themes that might be holding the company back from being as effective as it can be in attracting and retaining great talent. Asking these questions requires an open mind and thick skin, but the payoff can be huge. And just by asking, the company gains credibility with its constituents by showing that it is self-reflective and committed to improvement.

# The Gracious Recruiter

At the most basic level, candidates want to be treated well, communicated with, and respected. Whether your message is, "Welcome aboard," "Your qualifications don't match our needs," or, "You are a great candidate, but the timing is wrong," the way these messages are communicated is important to the candidate, the company, and to the success of the recruiter herself. "Gracious recruiting" is the principle that everyone who shows a level of interest in your company should be treated with courtesy. Courtesy and graciousness involve all of the simple, small acts that we sometimes forget about but that can have huge implications in the marketplace for great talent.

Over time, because companies have not made talent the competitive priority that it should be, candidates have learned to expect the cold shoulder from HR departments and recruiters. They do not expect any action, and they do everything they can to bypass these "screeners" and get straight to the hiring decision maker.

It is unfortunate that courtesy has become a differentiator, but as a result, a little graciousness goes a long way. From the first greeting, whether on the Web site, at a trade fair, or elsewhere, a gracious message will form a foundation for a relationship of goodwill.

A gracious recruiter is honest with himself and others. He takes the time to ask questions and fully understand the needs of every participant in the hiring process. He provides great service, responding immediately to the needs of all his constituencies. He returns value to all candidates, regardless of whether they meet the company's needs, by explaining the process and even spending time with rejected candidates when possible to help them grow and develop. Instead of asking, "What do you do?" the gracious recruiter asks, "What do you want to do, and how can we help?"

A recruiter is not only the face of your new talent organization, but also the face of your company. Each new applicant is not only potential Q-Talent, but also a potential customer, partner, investor, and evangelist. In a world where a lot of people inside of companies have simply forgotten how to treat others the right way, the recruiter who approaches his or her relationships with graciousness and a spirit of service makes a noticeable difference and introduces another way to help differentiate the company over time.

Life is too short to treat people any other way. If there is only one thing you take away from this chapter, we want it to be this: *Be gracious.* Your candidates will benefit, your company will benefit, and, as a recruiter whose livelihood depends on developing trusting, caring relationships, you will surely benefit, too.

# 9

# TALENT FORCES
# OF TOMORROW

---

*Forces in Play:* Changes in behavior, technology, demographics,
natural resources, and other areas force businesses to
continually look ahead and adapt. Wherever talent scarcity
takes hold, recruiting innovation responds. The most
competitive organizations will be leaders in this space.

The only constant in the business world is *change*. When the next big change comes for your business, will you have the talent you need to respond?

In addition to everything already on her plate, your Chief Talent Officer must wear one additional "hat." To keep your organization ahead of new forces and fluctuations in the talent market, your Chief Talent Officer must also be, to some extent, a futurist.

This does not mean you need to go out and hire the next H.G. Wells. But, just as the Chief Talent Officer must be well-grounded in the realities of the business she supports, she must also have an eye for what is unfolding beyond the walls of the company.

Many of the ideas discussed in this book will help your organization tackle the changing talent landscape and meet your need for Q-Talent today. But what about changes in the next 5 to 10 years and beyond? What are they, and how can you begin to respond today?

This chapter goes beyond the trends described in Chapter 2, "Talent Market Demands," to make several more far-reaching predictions that will affect the talent market for years to come. Many of the technologies and processes discussed in this chapter exist today but are not yet widely accepted or used, especially in the United States. Countries that are not bound by legacy technologies or processes might be the first to create and use technology for recruitment in new, interesting, and more effective ways. Pay attention to how recruiting evolves in emerging markets, such as China, and technology-saturated markets, such as Japan and Korea. The competition for Q-Talent is global, and some of the most innovative ideas for capturing Q-Talent might originate outside of your own country's borders.

# Internet Job Postings Go the Way of Newspaper Classifieds

They might feel "new" to many companies, but outside of convenience, Internet job postings do not offer much that newspapers have not been offering for decades. Online and newspaper classified advertisements have been "good enough" for many companies, but in a world of intensified competition for Q-Talent, static, uninteresting job descriptions posted at company and job search Web sites will not attract enough attention from prospective Q-Talent.

The ineffectiveness of both print and online classified ads will place increasing pressure on the traditional newspaper business model, where advertisements, including classified ads, drive the business. Many newspapers are already struggling to find a new Internet-based model that can replace this traditional advertising "cash cow." "Roll-up" strategies, including consolidation, will occur, and new business models will emerge.

Remember, companies competing for talent need to unlock the "passive candidate" talent pool. Classified ads have never been the best way to reach passive candidates, individuals who are happy in their current positions but are open to considering other compelling opportunities. With abundant labor supplies of the past, companies have been able to find someone at just about any time for just about any opening. Rarely have they assigned anyone with great marketing expertise to help with job postings.

No more. The idea of talent brands described in Chapter 4, "The Cultural Obsession of Work," leading to rich, interactive, informative, and attractive job- and company-related information targeted at Q-Talent is about to take a huge leap. Niche job boards and selective talent communities will increase in popularity as they provide a more effective way for both companies and Q-Talent to find each other. Just as commercial media is being splintered by myriad communication formats, including an explosion of cable channels, Web sites, and blogs, static classified ads will be surpassed by interactive pods, blogs, and feeds.

## Podcasting, VCasts, and Feeds

As with all new technologies, adoption occurs in phases. Each phase will bring innovations to the way you attract and secure Q-Talent. Throughout this book, we have shown how technology that is in widespread use today, such as e-mail, Web sites, blogs, and chat rooms, already affects your ability to hire Q-Talent. Companies, including IBM, Microsoft, and others, maintain blogs written and managed by their own employees that provide information about company culture, projects, and opportunities. Companies are capturing relationships by asking for prospective candidates' e-mail addresses and using them to open a dialogue, create relationships, and build talent communities of future Q-Talent prospects, as described in Chapter 5, "Building a Talent Community."

Efforts to build talent communities will be aided by file formats, such as Really Simple Syndication (RSS), which enables you to syndicate your content. Just about any kind of information on the Web can be broken down and "broadcast" via RSS. Users "tune in" to the RSS feeds in which they are interested. The feeds are updated whenever changes are made to the Web pages a person is monitoring.

People who want to learn more about open positions at a particular company can fill out a profile of their career interests and ask to receive news of positions that match those interests through an RSS channel, or "feed." Any time a position is posted that matches their interests, they receive an "alert" that the information has been automatically downloaded, allowing them to respond quickly if interested. In this way, companies can communicate with their talent communities almost instantly. A few Web sites are already doing this today, and many more will likely be doing it between 2005 and 2010.

Another way to add value to a company's blogs and Web sites is with "podcasting." First developed by former MTV vee-jay Adam Curry in 2004, a podcast is an audio file that can be automatically downloaded, stored, and listened to using an MP3 player, such as an iPod. (The term *podcasting* is a combination of the words *iPod* and *broadcasting*.) Curry saw the huge potential in blogs and wanted to add audio to them. He teamed with one of the founders of RSS, and yet another new communications format was born. Curry now uses podcasting to broadcast his radio show to a growing audience. No radio, no satellite, just an audio blog delivered to listeners.

Podcasting, too, will make its way into the talent arena. For example, some Internet job postings will become audio descriptions from the recruiter, the hiring manager, or even the CEO. This will enable companies to convey their passion and sense of urgency about an open position through the voices of real people. It will add depth and emotion to one of the most emotional processes we engage in throughout our lives—the search for work.

Podcasting is likely to expand to video, and with integrated telephony slowly realizing its promise, companies will deliver job descriptions to candidates' phones, too. Prospective talent will have the option to receive audio position descriptions by phone or via the Internet. The telephone approach will also be interactive, allowing the candidate to submit a profile, answer questions, receive instructions, and perhaps even have the option to speak directly with a recruiter.

The capability of cell phones to transmit both voice and nonvoice data has given rise to "VCasts," short broadcast television episodes created for viewing on mobile phone screens. In late 2004, Fox TV announced plans to create VCasts and broadcast them via the Vodaphone and Verizon networks.

As companies form relationships with prospective talent via their talent communities (see Chapter 5), they will strive to provide prospective talent with information of interest. VCasts will be another channel for doing so, with the ability to provide videos about a special job, company vignettes, CEO presentations, and other information conducive to this format.

For example, suppose that an accountant is leaving Manhattan by train for the 90-minute commute home. He checks his cell phone for messages and sees that he has one inviting him to view a VCast on a job opportunity that matches his interests. Is he likely to view it? Yes. Does it spark his interest in the position? Possibly.

As an extension of this capability, savvy talent organizations that understand the value of these relationships will partner with their marketing colleagues to launch joint marketing efforts that match candidates' interests with relevant products and services in a way that benefits both parties. This opportunity will provide another way for the talent organization to drive revenue and evolve from "overhead" to become another profit center.

The convergence of all media channels—cable television, the Internet, and radio—is driving new content creation and delivery and the business models to support them. These developments will have a particularly profound impact in parts of Asia, where personal computers are relatively rare and most of the "wired" population instead accesses the Internet via cellular telephones. If the economies in some Asian countries take off the way many expect, there will be high demand for talent, leading to the growth of the recruiting industry there and innovative approaches to acquiring talent.

## The Advertising/Marketing Force Meets the Talent Force

Madison Avenue is managed by executives still living in a 1950s advertising world, pushing advertising concepts from the 1970s at talent living in the early twenty-first century. This model must change. Already, largely due to technology, the way we create and deliver advertising and marketing messages is changing—quickly.

Creating and delivering effective recruiting messages requires new thinking, new technology, and changes in the way companies use traditional recruitment marketing dollars. Again, this area offers an opportunity for talent organizations to add value to the business by generating great talent *and* increased profits.

Let's revisit the concept of talent communities. Many companies have already accumulated thousands of relationships through their career Web sites. Visitors have "opted-in," agreeing to receive information on the company or its industry. What type of information are these people interested in receiving from you? Chapter 5 provided some examples. Are they poised to participate in a project, if asked? Are they poised to buy?

If your organization wants to increase sales before the end of the quarter, would your talent community be responsive to a special offer on certain products? What if the offer included a discount on future products or a "buy-one-get-one-free" proposition?

Some talent organizations will carry these messages even further. When people register online, some might indicate interest in executive-level job openings. Demographic research would reveal that people interested in these positions drive certain cars, take unique vacations, look for special homes, and so forth. Based on this information, in addition to its job-related messages, the company might offer a special on a Calloway Driver, for example, to selected members of their talent community.

Earlier, we described VCasts. In addition to providing compelling content via VCasts, companies might offer incentives for people to view them. This way, the company secures an audience and perhaps piques the interest of some Q-Talent while viewers get something in return such as a free product or an offer to participate in a drawing for a great vacation.

Done correctly, by respecting members' privacy and carefully targeting the offer to their expressed interests, these efforts can help the company provide something of value as they work to build talent relationships.

In an economy where targeted marketing is vital to success, many companies will find a treasure trove of data and relationships right under their nose in their talent community profiles. If you are in a talent organization, talk to your marketing counterpart about the potential value of the people who visit your careers site and develop a strategy for how to capture and nurture these relationships.

If you are in marketing, invite your organization's talent leader to work with you to drive revenue through their department.

And if you lead a company, recognize that your talent and marketing organizations share a goal to sell your company to their respective audiences. Challenge these organizations to work together to achieve long-term company goals. Encourage them to abandon legacy processes and try new, creative approaches. Give them a timeline and make it clear how you will measure their success.

Beyond the efforts you pursue within your company, a new industry designed to advertise and market to Q-Talent will develop and thrive. New concepts that provide more targeted marketing and recruiting initiatives will yield better results for companies and talent alike.

## The Television Industry "Gets It": Just About Everyone Works

Chapter 4 described how work and the pursuit of work is increasingly a cultural obsession. Work, jobs, and improving our economic lives will become even more ingrained in the public consciousness than they are today. In much of the industrialized world, television is also a big part of the public consciousness. So it is not surprising that much of what people see in their living rooms every night on TV deals with the world of work and careers in some way.

How will a burgeoning recruitment industry take advantage of this medium? One group in Southern California created the Career Entertainment Channel to deliver cable TV programming about work. Taking this simple idea one step further, an organization could create an ecosystem of television programming about jobs, careers, and the pursuit of better jobs and careers.

A careers network will emerge—the "early MTV" of career-related programming—that delivers not only entertainment but also information, news, and content that brings employers and talent together. It might feature the following:

- A career-and-business news show, such as ESPN's *SportsCenter*, delivered multiple times per day

- A career biographies show profiling well-known business leaders and their career moves

- A business version of Bravo's *Inside the Actor's Studio*, where a prominent business school dean could interview well-known business professionals and students could ask questions in a real-time, open classroom setting

- Reality shows that build off NBC's *The Apprentice* and depict job candidates or new hires experiencing a job search, interview, or on-the-job training

A careers network is also a natural place to join the two most powerful media in the world: television and the Internet. This type of programming would provide a compelling reason for viewers to go back and forth between their television and the Web. As discussed earlier in this chapter, VCasts are already combining TV programming with cell phone delivery. Companies, including content providers and advertisers, will take advantage of this convergence. The demographic for career-related TV programming is as focused as they come. Any company interested in reaching out to job seekers will have a new sweet spot for their advertising dollars. The network's online integration could also be a revenue generator. For example, VCasts of one reality television show were expected to cost between 50 and 90 cents to download. Micro-transactions will merge with new methods of content delivery to provide new forms of revenue.

## Talent Personalization

Personalization technology will continue to mature far beyond recommending CDs and books. Web sites, such as Amazon and Google, already have personalization technologies that model our behavior and serve up targeted advertising. We already carry a great deal of personal information around on our credit cards—even your gas station knows who you are. When you combine portable, personal information with emerging technologies, such as Wi-Fi, radio frequency ID tags, content management and personalization software, customer relationship management software, GPS devices; and future technologies, such as information-encoded smart chips, smaller Flash-memory devices, and retina scans, the possibilities are staggering.

Personalization is a form of artificial intelligence. For many business applications, personalization provides a way of knowing about an individual—his interests, needs, past behavior, and skills—and using that information to provide relevant products and services. Personalization raises privacy concerns that need to be addressed. However, as new technology protects us from privacy violations, personalization will become a bigger part of our everyday lives, including how we will manage our careers and jobs. How will personalization affect the talent market?

Personalization will allow job-related information to be provided in a more targeted way. For example, when someone uses search engines, such as Yahoo! and Google, relevant job listings will be exposed based on personalized data the searcher has provided. For example, if someone searches for a medical report and has revealed via his personalized data that he is a doctor, the site can provide search results, as well as additional links to relevant boards or companies. A truck driver obtaining route maps via Mapquest might receive targeted offers or other information based on his position and the areas where he travels.

Other near-term advances might help bring about far-reaching results in the quest for Q-Talent. Japan and some Scandinavian countries are starting to use cell phones as credit cards. Shoppers hold phones up to an electronic sensor, enter a personal ID number, and their card is charged for purchases made. This is a growing industry, and many believe that the cellular phone will evolve to perform many functions beyond communications, becoming a repository for personal information, much like an electronic wallet.

Another twist on the electronic wallet idea is that credit cards will evolve to serve this purpose. Micro-transactions, where the billing for small credit card purchases (such as 99-cent song downloads) are held and bundled together for one transaction at the end of the billing cycle, allow people in emerging countries to use credit cards. This might be the last barrier to the piece of plastic becoming the place where we carry our resumés, profiles, and life stories. And with a swipe or a pass-through, we can choose to let someone else know what we do for a living—and what we would *like* to do for a living.

Using a bit of imagination, what if those interested in fielding new job offers could program their electronic wallet—whether a cell phone, credit card, or other device—allowing recruiters to access this information and approach them with relevant opportunities? As the candidate, you might be standing in a hotel lobby and someone would approach you, already knowing what you do for a living and your job search criteria, and ask whether you would be open to doing something else, which, according to the information you have made available, could be a perfect fit. When you attend a tradeshow or job fair, you could swipe your card upon entry, making the event a much more two-way experience, as you not only seek out people of interest, but they seek you out, too.

There are many science-fiction-like scenarios for how recruiting might evolve. In the film *Minority Report*, the character John Anderton, played by Tom Cruise, has personal information embedded in his retina. In one scene, as he walks down a street, holographic advertisements scan his retina and access a database to find out who he is and what he has purchased. In response, female images, most likely ones that meet his interest, deliver personalized and suggestive messages.

Today, retina scan technology is being tested in airports in Germany. With an aging population and an economy that is looking to reinvent itself, Germany might need to recruit Q-Talent outside its borders. When retina scan technology matures, Germany would have the capability to immediately know where new arrivals are from, and in some cases what they do, as they are entering the country. Why wouldn't they market their great jobs and great lifestyle to visiting professionals? To make this type of marketing even more targeted, Germany could ask visitors to proclaim their work title on their visa. Each professional entering the country could also be entered into a countrywide talent database. Certain companies or government organizations might even have priorities set up within the program.

With this system, when a prospective candidate visits Oktoberfest and walks by a tourism display, his or her cell phone or retina could be scanned, and job-related invitations or opportunities could be delivered by a German model guaranteed to catch the person's eye.

The key to unlocking the potential of these technologies is to find a balance between their capabilities and the standards and expectations of human interaction. Most likely, laws will be required to protect individuals from those who would abuse these capabilities. For example, privacy laws might require that visitors be allowed to "opt-in" to personalization systems and require companies to ask for permission before capturing personal information about its customers or using that information to provide personalized shopping or other services.

## The Force of Change

Our work defines us, gives us sustenance, and provides meaning in our lives by allowing us to contribute to the greater good. The reasons that we work might not change, but the way the work, where we work, and why we work are changing dramatically. Our talent—properly applied, developed, and managed—is the foundation of success for us and our organizations, companies, and nations.

In the Introduction, we shared a biblical parable about talent. The story asked a question that we ask again today: Do we figure out how to take one talent and turn it into 10, or do we bury our talent in the ground to protect what we have? Developing our talent and putting it to the best possible use is part of what it means to be human. To reach our full potential as individuals, organizations, and countries, we must embrace our talents every day. As organizations, we must act now to make sure that we have the right people at all levels of our company and that we will continue to have the talent force we need for years to come.

We choose whether to develop our talent and how to apply it. We choose to find solutions to challenges or to accept the status quo. It is time to accept the charter to use our talent as individuals, companies, and nations to promote good and to find solutions for greater prosperity and peace. No matter who we are, where we live, or our chronological age . . . it's time. What an awesome challenge. Let's begin.

"The best time to plant a tree is 20 years ago. The second best time is now."

—Ancient Chinese proverb

Peace, health, and happiness.

# INDEX

Check out…


*Why Great Leaders Don't Take Yes for an Answer*
*Answer*
*Managing for Conflict and Consensus*


**Michael A. Roberto**

ISBN: 0-13-145439-0
$29.95
©2005 Pearson Education, Inc.

**Here's a sneak peek of Chapter 1…**

# 1

# THE LEADERSHIP
# CHALLENGE

**"Diversity in counsel, unity in command."**

**—Cyrus the Great**

In February 2003, the Columbia space shuttle disintegrated while re-entering the earth's atmosphere. In May 1996, Rob Hall and Scott Fischer, two of the world's most accomplished mountaineers, died on the slopes of Everest along with three of their clients during the deadliest day in the mountain's history. In April 1985, the Coca-Cola Company changed the formula of its flagship product and enraged its most loyal customers. In April 1961, a brigade of Cuban exiles invaded the Bay of Pigs with the support of the United States government, and Fidel Castro's military captured or killed nearly the entire rebel force. Catastrophe and failure, whether in business, politics, or other walks of life, always brings forth many troubling questions. Why did NASA managers decide not to undertake corrective action when they discovered that a potentially dangerous foam debris strike had occurred during the launch of the Columbia space shuttle? Why did Hall and Fischer choose to ignore their own safety rules and procedures and push forward toward the summit of Mount Everest despite knowing that they would be forced to conduct a very dangerous nighttime descent? Why did Roberto Goizueta and his management team fail to anticipate the overwhelmingly negative public reaction to New Coke? Why did President John F. Kennedy decide to support a rebel invasion despite the existence of information that suggested an extremely low probability of success?

We ask these questions because we hope to learn from others' mistakes, and we do not wish to repeat them. Often, however, a few misconceptions about the nature of organizational decision making cloud our judgment and make it difficult to draw the appropriate lessons from these failures. Many of us have an image of how these failures transpire. We envision a chief executive, or a management team, sitting in a room one day making a fateful decision. We rush to find fault with the analysis that they conducted, wonder about their business acumen, and perhaps even question their motives. When others falter, we often search for flaws in others' intellect or personality. Yet, differences in mental horsepower seldom distinguish success from failure when it comes to strategic decision making in complex organizations.

What do I mean by strategic decision making? Strategic choices occur when the stakes are high, ambiguity and novelty characterize the situation, and the decision represents a substantial commitment of financial, physical, and/or human resources. By definition, these choices occur rather infrequently, and they have a potentially significant impact on an organization's future performance. They differ from routine or tactical choices that managers make each and every day, in which the problem is well-defined, the alternatives are clear, and the impact on the overall organization is rather minimal.[1]

Strategic decision making in a business enterprise or public sector institution is a dynamic process that unfolds over time, moves in fits and starts, and flows across multiple levels of an organization.[2] Social, political, and emotional forces play an enormous role. Whereas the cognitive task of decision making may prove challenging for many leaders, the socio-emotional component often proves to be a manager's Achilles' heel. Moreover, leaders not only must select the appropriate course of action, they need to mobilize and motivate the organization to implement it effectively. As Noel Tichy and Dave Ulrich write, "CEOs tend to overlook the lesson Moses learned several thousand years ago—namely, getting the ten commandments written down and communicated is the easy part; getting them implemented is the challenge."[3] Thus, decision-making success is a function of both decision quality and implementation effectiveness. Decision quality means that managers choose the course of action that enables the organization to achieve its objectives more efficiently than all other plausible alternatives. Implementation effectiveness means that the organization successfully carries out the selected course of action, thereby meeting the objectives established during the decision-making process. A central premise of this book is that a leader's ability to navigate his or her way through the personality clashes, politics, and social pressures of the decision process often determines whether managers will select the appropriate alternative and implementation will proceed smoothly.

Many executives can run the numbers or analyze the economic structure of an industry; a precious few can master the social and political dynamic of decision making. Consider the nature and quality of dialogue within many organizations. Candor, conflict, and debate appear conspicuously absent during their decision-making processes. Managers feel uncomfortable expressing dissent, groups converge quickly on a particular solution, and individuals assume that unanimity exists when, in fact, it does not. As a result, critical assumptions remain untested, and creative alternatives do not surface or receive adequate attention. In all too many cases, the problem begins with the person directing the process, as their words and deeds discourage

a vigorous exchange of views. Powerful, popular, and highly successful leaders hear "yes" much too often, or they simply hear nothing
when people really mean "no." In those situations, organizations may
not only make poor choices, but they may find that unethical choices
remain unchallenged. As *Business Week* declared in its 2002 special
issue on corporate governance, "The best insurance against crossing
the ethical divide is a roomful of skeptics...By advocating dissent, top
executives can create a climate where wrongdoing will not go unchallenged."[4]

Of course, conflict alone does not lead to better decisions.
Leaders also need to build consensus in their organizations.
Consensus, as we define it here, does *not* mean unanimity, widespread agreement on all facets of a decision, or complete approval by
a majority of organization members. It does *not* mean that teams,
rather than leaders, make decisions. Consensus *does* mean that people have agreed to cooperate in the implementation of a decision.
They have accepted the final choice, even though they may not be
completely satisfied with it. Consensus has two critical components: a
high level of commitment to the chosen course of action and a strong,
shared understanding of the rationale for the decision.[5] Commitment
helps to prevent the implementation process from becoming derailed
by organizational units or individuals who object to the selected
course of action. Moreover, commitment may promote management
perseverance in the face of other kinds of implementation obstacles,
while encouraging individuals to think creatively and innovatively
about how to overcome those obstacles. Common understanding of
the decision rationale allows individuals to coordinate their actions
effectively, and it enhances the likelihood that everyone will act in a
manner that is "consistent with the spirit of the decision."[6] Naturally,
consensus does not ensure effective implementation, but it enhances
the likelihood that managers can work together effectively to overcome obstacles that arise during decision execution.

Commitment without deep understanding can amount to "blind
devotion" on the part of a group of managers. Individuals may accept

a call to action and dedicate themselves to the implementation of a particular plan, but they take action based on differing interpretations of the decision. Managers may find themselves working at cross-purposes, not because they want to derail the decision, but because they perceive goals and priorities differently than their colleagues. When leaders articulate a decision, they hope that subordinates understand the core intent of the decision, because people undoubtedly will encounter moments of ambiguity as they execute the plan of action. During these uncertain situations, managers need to make choices without taking the time to consult the leader or all other colleagues. Managers also may need to improvise a bit to solve problems or capitalize on opportunities that may arise during the implementation process. A leader cannot micromanage the execution of a decision; he needs people throughout the organization to be capable of making adjustments and trade-offs as obstacles arise; shared understanding promotes that type of coordinated, independent action.

Shared understanding without commitment leads to problems as well. Implementation performance suffers if managers comprehend goals and priorities clearly, but harbor doubts about the wisdom of the choice that has been made. Execution also lags if people do not engage and invest emotionally in the process. Managers need to not only comprehend their required contribution to the implementation effort, they must be willing to "go the extra mile" to solve difficult problems and overcome unexpected hurdles that arise.[7]

Unfortunately, if executives engage in vigorous debate during the decision process, people may walk away dissatisfied with the outcome, disgruntled with their colleagues, and not fully dedicated to the implementation effort. Conflict may diminish consensus, and thereby hinder the execution of a chosen course of action, as Figure 1-1 illustrates. Herein lies a fundamental dilemma for leaders: How does one foster conflict and dissent to enhance decision quality while simultaneously building the consensus required to implement decisions effectively? In short, how does one achieve "diversity in counsel, unity in command?" The purpose of this book is to help leaders tackle this daunting challenge.

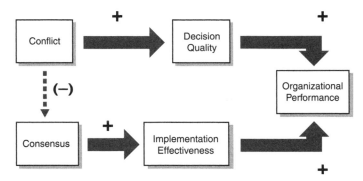

**FIGURE 1-1:   The effects of conflict and consensus**

# Decision-Making Myths

When we read about a CEO's failed strategy in *Business Week*, or analyze the actions of the manager profiled in a case study at Harvard Business School, we often ask ourselves: How could that individual make such a stupid decision? My students ask themselves this question on numerous occasions each semester as they read about companies that falter or fold. Perhaps we think of others' failures in these terms because of our hubris, or because we might need to convince ourselves that we can succeed when embarking upon similar endeavors fraught with ambiguity and risk. Jon Krakauer, a member of Rob Hall's 1996 Everest expedition, wrote, "If you can convince yourself that Rob Hall died because he made a string of stupid errors and that you are too clever to repeat those errors, it makes it easier for you to attempt Everest in the face of some rather compelling evidence that doing so is injudicious."[8]

Let's examine a few of our misconceptions about decision making in more detail and attempt to distinguish myth from reality. (See Table 1-1 for a summary of these common myths.) Can we, in fact, attribute the failure to a particular individual, namely the CEO, president, or expedition leader? Does the outcome truly suggest a lack of intelligence, industry expertise, or technical knowledge on the part of key participants? Did the failure originate with one particular flawed decision or should we examine a pattern of choices over time?

**TABLE 1-1:   Myth Versus Reality in Strategic Decision Making**

| Myth | Reality |
| --- | --- |
| The chief executive decides. | Strategic decision making entails simultaneous activity by people at multiple levels of the organization. |
| Decisions are made in the room. | Much of the real work occurs "offline," in one-on-one conversations or small subgroups, not around a conference table. |
| Decisions are largely intellectual exercises. | Strategic decisions are complex social, emotional, and political processes. |
| Managers analyze and then decide. | Strategic decisions unfold in a nonlinear fashion, with solutions frequently arising before managers define problems or analyze alternatives. |
| Managers decide and then act. | Strategic decisions often evolve over time and proceed through an iterative process of choice and action. |

## Myth 1: The Chief Executive Decides

When Harry Truman served as president of the United States, he placed a sign on his desk in the Oval Office. It read *The Buck Stops Here*. The now-famous saying offers an important reminder for all leaders. The CEO bears ultimate responsibility for the actions of his or her firm, and the president must be accountable for the policies of his administration. However, when we examine the failures of large, complex organizations, we ought to be careful before we assume that poor decisions are the work of a single actor, even if that person serves as the powerful and authoritative chief executive of the institution.

A great deal of research dispels the notion that CEOs or presidents make most critical decisions on their own. Studies show that bargaining, negotiating, and coalition building among managers shape the decisions that an organization makes. The decision-making process often involves managers from multiple levels of the organization, and it does not proceed in a strictly "bottom-up" or "top-down" fashion. Instead, activity occurs simultaneously at multiple levels of the organization. The decision-making process becomes quite diffuse in some instances.[9] For example, in one study of foreign policy decision making, political scientist Graham Allison concluded that, "Large acts result from innumerable and often conflicting smaller actions by individuals at various levels of organization in the service of a variety of only partially compatible conceptions of national goals, organizational goals, and political objectives."[10] In short, the chief executive may make the ultimate call, but that decision often emerges from a process of intense interaction among individuals and subunits throughout the organization.

### Myth 2: Decisions Are Made in the Room

Many scholars and consultants have argued that a firm's strategic choices emerge from deliberations among members of the "top management team." However, this concept of a senior team may be a bit misleading.[11] As management scholar Donald Hambrick wrote, "Many top management 'teams' may have little 'teamness' to them. If so, this is at odds with the implicit image...of an executive conference table where officers convene to discuss problems and make major judgments."[12]

In most organizations, strategic choices do not occur during the chief executive's staff meetings with his direct reports. In James Brian Quinn's research, he reported than an executive once told him, "When I was younger, I always conceived of a room where all these [strategic] concepts were worked out for the whole company. Later, I didn't find any such room."[13] In my research, I have found that crucial conversations occur "offline"—during one-on-one interactions and informal meetings of subgroups. People lobby their colleagues or superiors prior to meetings, and they bounce ideas off one another before presenting proposals to the entire management team. Managers garner commitment from key constituents prior to taking a public stance on an issue. Formal staff meetings often become an occasion for ratifying choices that have already been made, rather than a forum for real decision making.[14]

## Myth 3: Decisions Are Largely Intellectual Exercises

Many people think of decision making as a largely cognitive endeavor. In school and at work, we learn that "smart" people think through issues carefully, gather data, conduct comprehensive analysis, and then choose a course of action. Perhaps they apply a bit of intuition and a few lessons from experience as well. Poor decisions must result from a lack of intelligence, insufficient expertise in a particular domain, or a failure to conduct rigorous analysis. Psychologists offer a slightly more forgiving explanation for faulty choices. They find that all of us—expert or novice, professor or student, leader or follower—suffer from certain cognitive biases. In other words, we make systematic errors in judgment, rooted in the cognitive, information-processing limits of the human brain, that impair our decision making.[15] For instance, most human beings are susceptible to the "sunk-cost bias"—the tendency to escalate commitment to a flawed and risky course of action if one has made a substantial prior investment of time, money, and other resources. We fail to recognize that the sunk costs should be irrelevant when deciding whether to move forward, and therefore, we throw "good money after bad" in many instances.[16]

Cognition undoubtedly plays a major role in decision making. However, social pressures become a critical factor at times. People have a strong need to belong—a desire for interpersonal attachment. At times, we feel powerful pressures to conform to the expectations or behavior of others. Moreover, individuals compare themselves to others regularly, often in ways that reflect favorably on themselves. These social behaviors shape and influence the decisions that organizations make. Emotions also play a role. Individuals appraise how proposed courses of action might affect them, and these assessments arouse certain feelings. These emotions can energize and motivate individuals, or they can lead to resistance or paralysis. Finally, political behavior permeates many decision-making processes, and it can have positive or negative effects. At times, coalition building, lobbying, bargaining, and influence tactics enhance the quality of decisions that are ultimately made; in other instances, they lead to suboptimal outcomes.[17] Without a doubt, leaders ignore these social, emotional, and political forces at their own peril.

### Myth 4: Managers Analyze and Then Decide

At one point or another, most of us have learned structured problem-solving techniques. A typical approach consists of five well-defined phases: 1) identify and define the problem, 2) gather information and data, 3) identify alternative solutions, 4) evaluate each of the options, 5) select a course of action. In short, we learn to analyze a situation in a systematic manner and then make a decision. Unfortunately, most strategic decision processes do not unfold in a linear fashion, passing neatly from one phase to the next.[18] Activities such as alternative evaluation, problem definition, and data collection often occur in parallel, rather than sequentially. Multiple process iterations take place, as managers circle back to redefine problems or gather more information even after a decision has seemingly been made. At times, solutions even arise in search of problems to solve.[19]

In my research, I have found that managers often select a preferred course of action, and *then* employ formal analytical techniques to evaluate various alternatives. What's going on here? Why does analysis follow choice in certain instances? Some managers arrive a decision intuitively, but they want to "check their gut" using a more systematic method of assessing the situation. Others use the analytics as a tool of persuasion when confronting skeptics or external constituencies, or because they must conform to cultural norms within the organization. Finally, many managers employ analytical frameworks for symbolic reasons. They want to signal that they have employed a thorough and logical decision-making process. By enhancing the perceived legitimacy of the process, they hope to gain support for the choice that they prefer.[20]

Consider the story of the Ford Mustang—one of the most remarkable and surprising new product launches in auto-industry history. Lee Iacocca's sales and product design instincts told him that the Mustang would be a smashing success in the mid-1960s, but much to his chagrin, he could not persuade senior executives to produce the car. Iacocca recognized that quantitative data analysis trumped intuition in the intensively numbers-driven culture created by former Ford executive Robert McNamara. Thus, Iacocca set out to marshal quantitative evidence, based on market research, which suggested that the Mustang would attract enough customers to justify the capital investment required to design and manufacture the car. Not surprisingly, Iacocca's analysis supported his initial position! Having produced data to support his intuition, Iacocca prevailed in his battle to launch the Mustang.[21]

The nonlinear nature of strategic decision making may seem dysfunctional at first glance. It contradicts so much of what we have learned or teach in schools of business and management. However, multiple iterations, feedback loops, and simultaneous activity need not be dysfunctional. A great deal of learning and improvement can occur as a decision process proceeds in fits and starts. Some nonlinear processes may be fraught with dysfunctional political behavior, but without a doubt, effective decision making involves a healthy dose of reflection, revision, and learning over time.

### *Myth 5: Managers Decide and Then Act*

Consider the case of a firm apparently pursuing a diversification strategy. We might believe that executives made a choice at a specific point in time to enter new markets or seek growth opportunities beyond the core business. In reality, however, we may not find a clear starting or ending point for that decision process. Instead, the diversification decision may have evolved over time, as multiple parties investigated new technologies, grappled with declining growth in the core business, and considered how to invest excess cash flow. Executives might have witnessed certain actions taking place at various points in the organization and then engaged in a process of retrospective sense making, interpretation, and synthesis.[22] From this interplay between thought and action, a "decision" emerged.[23]

In my research, I studied an aerospace and defense firm's decision to invest more than $200 million in a new shipbuilding facility; the project completely transformed the organization's manufacturing process. When asked about the timing of the decision, one executive commented to me, "The decision to do this didn't come in November of 1996, it didn't come in February of 1997, it didn't come in May of 1997. You know, there was a concept, and the concept evolved." The implementation process did not follow neatly after a choice had been made. Instead, actions pertaining to the execution of the decision become intermingled with the deliberations regarding whether and how to proceed. The project gained momentum over time, and by the time the board of directors met to formally approve the project, everyone understood that the decision had already been made.

# Managing Reality

When Jack Welch took over as CEO of General Electric, he exhorted his managers to "face reality…see the world the way it is, not the way you wish it were."[24] This advice certainly applies to the challenge of managing high-stakes decision-making processes in complex and dynamic organizations. Leaders need to understand how decisions actually unfold so that they can shape and influence the process to their advantage. To cultivate conflict and build consensus effectively, they must recognize that the decision process unfolds across multiple levels of the organization, not simply in the executive suite. They need to welcome divergent views, manage interpersonal disagreements, and build commitment across those levels. Leaders also need to recognize that they cannot remove politics completely from the decision process, somehow magically transforming it into the purely intellectual exercise that they wish it would become. As Joseph Bower wrote, "politics is not pathology; it is a fact of large organization."[25] Effective leaders use political mechanisms to help them build consensus among multiple constituencies. Moreover, leaders cannot ignore the fact that managers often perform analyses to justify a preferred solution, rather than proceeding sequentially from problem identification to alternative evaluation to choice. Leaders must identify when such methods of persuasion become dysfunctional, and then intervene appropriately to maintain the legitimacy of the process, if they hope to build widespread commitment to a chosen course of action. With this organizational reality in mind, let's turn to the first element of Cyrus the Great's wise advice for decision makers: namely, the challenge of cultivating constructive conflict.

# The Absence of Dissent

How many of you have censored your views during a management meeting? Have you offered a polite nod of approval as your boss or a respected colleague puts forth a proposal, while privately harboring serious doubts? Have you immediately begun to devise ways to alter or reverse the decision at a later date?

If you have answered "yes" to these questions, be comforted by the fact that you are not alone. Many groups and organizations shy away from vigorous conflict and debate. For starters, managers often feel uncomfortable expressing dissent in the presence of a powerful, popular, and highly successful chief executive. It becomes difficult to be candid when the boss' presence dominates the room. We also find ourselves deferring to the technical experts in many instances, rather than challenging the pronouncements of company or industry veterans. Certain deeply held assumptions about customers, markets, and competition can become so in-grained in people's thought processes that an entire industry finds itself blindly accepting the prevailing conventional wisdom. Pressures for conformity also arise because cohesive, relatively homogenous groups of like-minded people have worked with one another for a long time.[26] Finally, some leaders engage in conflict avoidance because they do not feel comfortable with confrontation in a public setting. Whatever the reasons—and they are bountiful—the absence of healthy debate and dissent frequently leads to faulty decisions. Let's turn to a tragic example to see this dynamic in action.[27]

## Tragedy on Everest

In 1996, Rob Hall and Scott Fischer each led a commercial expedition team attempting to climb Mount Everest. Each group consisted of the leader, several guides, and eight paying clients. Although many team members reached the summit on May 10, they encountered grave dangers during their descent. Five individuals, including the two highly talented leaders, perished as they tried to climb down the mountain during a stormy night.

Many survivors and mountaineering experts have pointed out that the two leaders made a number of poor decisions during this tragedy. Perhaps most importantly, the groups ignored a critical decision rule created to protect against the dangers of descending after nightfall. Climbers typically begin their final push to the summit from a camp located at an altitude of about 26,000 feet (7,900 meters). They climb through the night, hoping to reach the summit by midday. Then, they scramble back down to camp, striving to reach the safety of their tents before sunset. This tight 18-hour schedule leaves little room for error. If climbers fall behind during the ascent, they face an extremely perilous nighttime descent. Hall and Fischer recognized these dangers. Moreover, they understood that individuals would find it difficult to abandon their summit attempt after coming so tantalizingly close to achieving their goal. They knew that climbers, as they near the summit, are particularly susceptible to the "sunk-cost bias." Thus, they advocated strict adherence to a predetermined decision rule. Fischer described it as the "two o'clock rule,"—i.e., when it became clear that a climber could not reach the top by two o'clock in the afternoon, that individual should abandon his summit bid and head back to the safety of the camp. If he failed to do so, the leaders and/or the guides should order the climbers to turn around. One team member recalled, "Rob had lectured us repeatedly about the importance of having a predetermined turnaround time on summit day…and abiding by it no matter how close we were to the top."[28]

Unfortunately, the leaders, guides, and most clients ignored the turnaround rule during the ascent. Nearly all the team members, including the two leaders, arrived at the summit after two o'clock. As a result, many climbers found themselves descending in darkness, well past midnight, as a ferocious blizzard enveloped the mountain. Not only did five people die, many others barely escaped with their lives.

Why did the climbers ignore the two o'clock rule? Many team members recognized quite explicitly the perils associated with violating the turnaround rule, but they chose not to question the leaders' judgment. The groups never engaged in an open and candid dialogue regarding the choice to push ahead. Neil Beidleman, a guide on Fischer's team, had serious reservations about climbing well past midday. However, he did not feel comfortable telling Fischer that the group should turn around. Perceptions of his relative status within the group affected Beidleman's behavior. He was "quite conscious of his place in the expedition pecking order," and consequently, he chose not to voice his concerns.[29] He reflected back, "I was definitely considered the third guide...so I tried not to be too pushy. As a consequence, I didn't always speak up when maybe I should have, and now I kick myself for it."[30] Similarly, Jon Krakauer, a journalist climbing as a member of Hall's team, began to sense the emergence of a "guide-client protocol" that shaped the climbers' behavior. Krakauer remarked, "On this expedition, he (Andy Harris—one of Rob Hall's guides) had been cast in the role of invincible guide, there to look after me and the other clients; we had been specifically indoctrinated not to question our guides' judgment."[31]

The climbers on these expedition teams also did not know one another very well. Many of them had not met their colleagues prior to arriving in Nepal. They found it difficult to develop mutual respect and trust during their short time together. Not knowing how others might react to their questions or comments, many climbers remained hesitant when doubts surfaced in their minds. Russian guide Anatoli Boukreev, who did not have a strong command of the English language, found it especially difficult to build relationships with his teammates. Consequently, he did not express his concerns about key aspects of the leaders' plans, for fear of how others might react to his opinions. Regretfully, he later wrote, "I tried not to be too argumentative, choosing instead to downplay my intuitions."[32]

Hall also made it clear to his team during the early days of the expedition that he would not welcome disagreement and debate during the ascent. He believed that others should defer to him because of his vast mountain-climbing expertise and remarkable track record of guiding clients to the summit of Everest. After all, Hall had guided a total of 39 clients to the top during 4 prior expeditions. He offered a stern pronouncement during the early days of the climb: "I will tolerate no dissension up there. My word will be absolute law, beyond appeal."[33] Hall made the statement because he wanted to preempt pushback from clients who might resist turning around if he instructed them to do so. Ironically, Hall fell behind schedule on summit day and should have turned back, but the clients did not challenge his decision to push ahead. Because of Hall's early declaration of authority, Krakauer concluded that, "Passivity on the part of the clients had thus been encouraged throughout our expedition."[34]

Before long, deference to the "experts" became a routine behavior for the team members. When the experts began to violate their own procedures or make other crucial mistakes, that pattern of deference persisted. Less-experienced team members remained hesitant to raise questions or concerns. Fischer's situation proved especially tragic. His physical condition deteriorated badly during the final summit push, and his difficulties became apparent to everyone including the relative novices. He struggled to put one foot in front of the other, yet "nobody discussed Fischer's exhausted appearance" or suggested that he should retreat down the slopes.[35]

Unfortunately, the experience of these teams on the slopes of Everest mirrors the group dynamic within many executive suites and corporate boardrooms in businesses around the world. The factors suppressing debate and dissent within these expedition teams also affect managers as they make business decisions. People often find themselves standing in Neil Beidleman's shoes—lower in status than other decision makers and unsure of the consequences of challenging those positioned on a higher rung in the organizational pecking order. Many leaders boast of remarkable track records, like Rob Hall, and employ an autocratic leadership style. Inexperienced individuals find themselves demonstrating excessive deference to those with apparent expertise in the subject at hand. Plenty of teams lack the atmosphere of mutual trust and respect that facilitates and encourages candid dialogue. Fortunately, most business decisions are not a matter of life or death.[36]

# The Perils of Conflict and Dissent

Of course, dissent does not always prove to be productive; cultivating conflict has its risks. To understand the perils, we must distinguish between two forms of conflict. Suppose that you ask your management team to compare and contrast two alternative courses of action. Individuals may engage in substantive debate over issues and ideas, which we refer to as cognitive, or task-oriented, conflict. This form of disagreement exposes each proposal's risks and weaknesses, challenges the validity of key assumptions, and even might encourage people to define the problem or opportunity confronting the firm in an entirely different light. For these reasons, cognitive conflict tends to enhance the quality of the solutions that groups produce. As former Intel CEO Andrew Grove once wrote, "Debates are like the process through which a photographer sharpens the contrast when developing a print. The clearer images that result permit management to make a more informed—and more likely correct—call."[37]

Unfortunately, when differences of opinion emerge during a discussion, managers may find it difficult to reconcile divergent views. At times, people become wedded to their ideas, and they begin to react defensively to criticism. Deliberations become heated, emotions flare, and disagreements become personal. Scholars refer to these types of personality clashes and personal friction as affective conflict. When it surfaces, decision processes often derail. Unfortunately, most leaders find it difficult to foster cognitive conflict without also stimulating interpersonal friction. The inability to disentangle the two forms of conflict has pernicious consequences. Affective conflict diminishes commitment to the choices that are made, and it disrupts the development of shared understanding. It also leads to costly delays in the decision process, meaning that organizations fail to make timely decisions, and they provide competitors with an opportunity to capture advantages in the marketplace.[38] Figure 1-2 depicts how cognitive and affective conflict shape decision-making outcomes.[39]

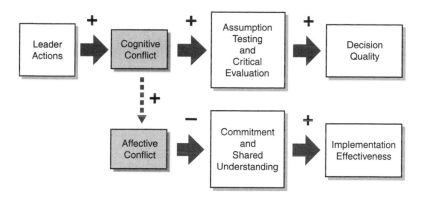

**FIGURE 1-2: Cognitive and affective conflict**

Consider the case of a defense electronics firm examining how to restructure a particular line of business. The chief executive wanted to take a hard look at the unit because it had become unprofitable. Multiple options emerged, and managers conducted a great deal of quantitative analysis to compare and contrast each possible course of action. A lively set of deliberations ensued. The chief financial officer played a particularly important role. He scrutinized all the proposals closely, treating each with equal skepticism. One manager remarked that, "He would be able to articulate the black and white logical reasons why things made sense, or why they didn't make sense...He was incredibly objective...like Spock on *Star Trek*." Unfortunately, not everyone could remain as objective. Some managers took criticism very personally during the deliberations, and working relationships became strained. Discussions became heated as individuals defended their proposals in which they had invested a great deal of time and energy. Some differences of opinion centered on a substantive issue; in other cases, people disagreed with one another simply because they did not want others to "win" the dispute. As one executive commented, "We could have put the legitimate roadblocks on the table, and separated those from the emotional roadblocks. We would have been much better off. But, we put them all in the same pot and had trouble sorting out which were real and which weren't." Ultimately, the organization made a decision regarding how to restructure, and looking back, nearly everyone agreed that they had discovered a creative and effective solution to the unit's problems. However, the organization struggled mightily to execute its chosen course of action in a timely and efficient manner. The entire implementation effort suffered from a lack of buy-in among people at various levels of the organization. Management overcame these obstacles and, eventually, the business became much more profitable. Nevertheless, the failure to develop a high level of consensus during the decision process cost the organization precious time and resources. Figure 1-3 depicts how conflict and consensus can come together to lead to positive outcomes rather than poor choices and flawed implementation efforts.

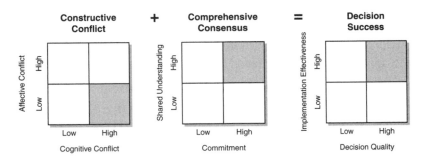

**FIGURE 1-3: The path to decision success**

# Why Is This So Difficult?

Why is managing conflict and building consensus so challenging? The roots of the problem may reside in one's style of leadership. Often, however, the difficulty reflects persistent patterns of dysfunction within groups and organizations. Let's try to understand a few sources of difficulty that leaders must overcome as they shape and direct decision processes.

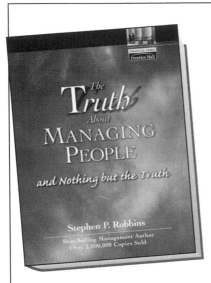

## The Truth About Managing People...And Nothing But the Truth

BY STEPHEN P. ROBBINS

This is a management book that cuts through the soft opinion and conjecture books that have dominated the business shelves in recent years and shows what management researchers know actually works, or doesn't work, when it comes to managing people. Contains over 60 proven "truths" that can transform how you manage people—and the results that are achieved.

ISBN 013066927X, © 2002, 240 pp., $19.00

## Why Great Leaders Don't Take Yes for an Answer
### Managing for Conflict and Consensus

BY MICHAEL A. ROBERTO

Executives hear "yes" far too often. Their status and power inhibits candid dialogue. They don't hear bad news until it's too late. They get groupthink, not reality. They think they've achieved consensus, then find their decisions undermined or derailed by colleagues who never really bought in. They become increasingly isolated; even high-risk or illegal actions can begin to go unquestioned. Inevitable? Absolutely not. In this book, Harvard Business School Professor Michael Roberto shows you how to promote honest, constructive dissent and skepticism...use it to improve your decisions...and then align your entire organization to fully support the decisions you make. Drawing on his extensive research on executive decision-making, Roberto shows how to test and probe the members of your management team...discover when "yes" means "yes" and when it doesn't...and build real, deep consensus that leads to action. Along the way, Roberto offers important new insights into managing teams, mitigating risk, promoting corporate ethics through effective governance, and much more. Your organization and your executive team have immense untapped wisdom: this book will help you tap that wisdom to the fullest.

ISBN 0131454390, © 2005, 304 pp., $29.95